T0283991

EYE

OF

ODIN

NORDIC MYTHOLOGY AND
THE WISDOM OF THE VIKINGS

ABOUT THE AUTHOR

PER HENRIK GULLFOSS has been teaching, consulting, and coaching in astrology and tarot for his entire adult life. A graduate of the University of Oslo, he has a master's degree in theater studies with honors in addition to his major in Religious History with a focus on Norse Mythology and Mysticism. In addition to these accomplishments, he is also a trained firewalking instructor. Per Henrik started the Nordic School of Astrology in 1992 and has many storied years of experience in teaching, consultations, coaching and lectures. He is also an ardent theater lover and has participated with many independent theater groups as an actor, director and playwright.

Over the years, Per has written 20 books on astrology being published internationally. He has also written several books on tarot, philosophy, reincarnation, mythology and the spiritual history of mankind, as well as a series of children's books in Norway. Many of his works have been translated into Danish, and several are considered classics in tarot and astrology.

Per Henrik Gullfoss has worked with alternative consciousness since 1980. Today, he trains astrologers and beginners who want to work with spiritual astrology and take a closer look at the soul's intention to incarnate on this planet. He is also co-editor and writer for the Norwegian magazine *Mystikk*.

You can also explore Nordic mythology further with participating in his class on www.udemy.com.

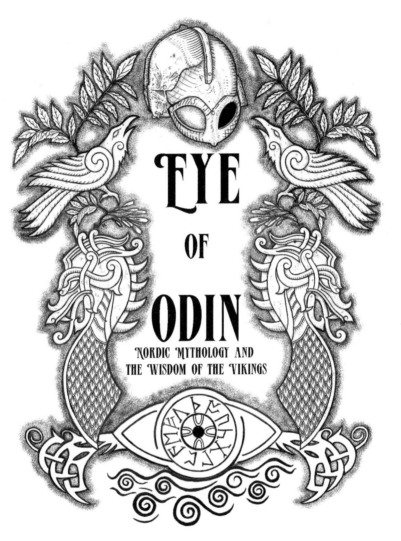

EYE

OF

ODIN

NORDIC MYTHOLOGY AND
THE WISDOM OF THE VIKINGS

PER HENRIK GULLFOSS

Chicago, Illinois

ISBN: 978-1-959883-25-8
Library of Congress Control Number on file.

Cover design by Leo Avila.
Edited by Becca Fleming.
Typesetting by Gianna Rini.

All images in this book are public domain.

Published by:
Crossed Crow Books, LLC
6934 N Glenwood Ave, Suite C
Chicago, IL 60626
www.crossedcrowbooks.com

Printed in the United States of America.

ACKNOWLEDGMENTS

This book came about through a long process, beginning when I was six years old and my grandfather gave me a leather-bound edition of Snorre's *Kings Sagas*. Over the next four years, I read that book eight times. With a history such as this, it comes as little surprise that *The Eye of Odin* should have come into being.

This book is not only for those who have a special interest in astrology or Norse mythology. It is for all who would like a greater understanding of the mythology from which they themselves come and for all who are open to a new way of understanding the world and human consciousness.

CONTENTS

4. Heimdall and Saturn • 61

5. Njord and Neptune • 73

6. Frey and Mars • 81

7. Freya and Venus • 89

8. Frigg and the Moon • 97

9. BALDER AND THE SUN • 101

10. RAGNARÖK • 113

FOREWORD

Many might know the tales of Norse mythology. How Thor and the Midgard serpent are forever locked in struggle, how the trickster Loki messes with plans, and how Odin attained his knowledge of the runes. In *The Eye of Odin,* Per takes us on a journey up and down the great World Tree, providing us with a guidebook to the inner and outer realms, one that works just as well as a map to Yggdrasil and the gods as it does to our own psyche and the stars above. He shines a new light on the world of the Vanir, Æsir, and all those who inhabit the worlds up and down the Tree. He takes us on a journey from the very beginning to the cosmic void of Ginnungagap through the words of the Völva and sagas, giving us comparisons to the classical planetary forces and astrology as well as figures from other pantheons. He flies us, like Huginn and Muninn, through the solar system, meeting gods and forces along the way, teaching us how classical astrology and Norse mythology go hand in hand.

This book is not a simple comparison but a new way of seeing the two through the same pair of eyes, helping us to deepen our perspective when working with planetary forces alongside the deities and spirits of Norse mythology. Per lays out for us the polarity and expressions of wisdom, either via the active and aggressive galdr (magic) of Odin or the passive and receptive seidr (magic) of the Norns, the Völva, and Freya. He then goes a step deeper, teaching us how we can work with the Norse mythological framework to also experience our inner universe. Like the body of Ymir makes up the physical world, so do the elements and primal forces make up our physical bodies. With the seat of our consciousness, the pinnacle throne of Odin is mirrored, from which we see and experience all worlds. Per shows us mythology as personal growth and tells us stories to teach us how to be, feel, see, and experience. This book works Norse mythology as a parable and a system of learning and enlightenment that aligns with that of classical astrology and, as such, the current of Western Occultism.

Per walks us through the outer worlds and how they mirror the inner and the great Yggdrasil, as our own psyche, its various inhabitants, seemingly independent, work together in harmony. He introduces us to familiar gods in new ways and helps us understand ourselves better in the process. He doesn't stop at the gods, giving us deeper breakdowns of some Nordic myths and legends, showing us how these stories are valuable lessons about life and our own behaviours. His comparison of the Norse pantheon with the astrological forces that influence our daily lives gives us a rich framework that we can use to approach the gods and begin to understand them as forces both within and without ourselves. Going beyond the likes of Joseph Cambell and Carl Jung, he breaks down Norse myth in a way that doesn't simply explain away aspects of these stories as simple psychology. Per gives us tools to understand these forces in a way that makes them accessible and relatable. As practitioners, this book becomes a tool for understanding both planetary forces and deities and becomes somewhat of a phonebook, showing us which beings may offer us appropriate help and expertise in times of need. Going deeper, this helps those of us who include deity in spell-work, learning that we can call upon Vanir and Æsir to lend help. With Per's help, we can travel the branches of Yggdrasil and meet with giants, dwarves, and Æsir alike, learning their secrets if we dare, knowing that we may not be the same person we once were when our journey began.

—Albert Björn Shiell, *Icelandic Plant Magic*

INTRODUCTION

Most of us are taught to view mythology as outdated or childish superstition, full of amusing stories and fairy tales. We are taught to see it as a primitive religion we can look back upon as being naive, a stage we've outgrown. The Christian Church has been very successful in ridding itself of mythology as a competitor by ridiculing all of it. It may seem as though Christianity, in its struggle against the heathens and toward a monopoly of the value of life, has succeeded in putting a lid on any attempt at meaningfully understanding Norse mythology. But now, much of what was hidden is about to emerge into the light.

Without knowing any better, you may have thought the old god-worshippers to be bearded, untamed barbarians, rather like a violent, savage youngster with a low brain capacity. At the same time, we who live in the Nordic parts of the world must admit to being proud of having these untamed wild beasts as our ancestors.

Let us look behind us and see what lies under the thousand-year layer of Christianity. To the astonishment of many, we find that the old north-dwellers were far from incompetent, believing the most foolish things. To worship a god who hangs on a cross seems, for the uninitiated, just as primitive and incomprehensible as parts of what Norse mythology can offer. A religion or mythology gives meaning only when we interpret the symbols on which it was built, thereby grasping what it was trying to say about the world.

A new interpretation of the Norse mythology is of particular importance today. It enables us to gain a new understanding of the culture we have grown away from. In other words, it is a valve by which we can contact a deeper and more collective layer of our psyche. In a time when we are effused with mystical knowledge from all corners of the earth, it is essential to contact our own source.

For those who work with and practice astrology, either professionally or as an amateur, such an insight into Norse mythology is of great importance, at least for those of us who live in northern latitudes. How we use the energies in a horoscope greatly depends on the environment we grew up in. In theory, a person born and bred in the Kalahari Desert and a Norwegian office clerk can have the same horoscope, but they will use and experience the energies in the horoscope differently.

As you might know, European astrology was born in the Middle East and was further developed by Mediterranean civilizations.[1] For this reason, in many languages, all the planets have names of Greek gods. In the northern parts of our globe, nature presents quite a different set of conditions to its inhabitants than the more temperate climate of the Mediterranean countries. Therefore, we have a very different relationship with the controlled and limiting energy that Saturn represents, for example. We are entirely dependent on solid and protective structures, such as warm houses, in order to survive.

In traditional astrology, Jupiter is often looked upon as being the lucky star—a bringer of luck and prosperity. But here in the cold north, we do not always look mildly upon those

---

1   Editors of Encyclopaedia Britannica. "Astrology Summary." *Encyclopedia Britannica*, 24 Jul. 2021.

who lay, laze, and receive without labor. Therefore, Jupiter is a far more demanding, vigorous, and harsh character here in the north than one is left to believe from reading astrological textbooks. We can compare our individual consciousness to an iceberg. We find a thousand-year history of Christian tradition just below the sea's surface. But under this, deeper levels lie, and among these, you find one stemming from Norse mythology. I will use an example to show how these deeper levels influence our attitudes to ourselves and the world around us.

In the Christian message, the demand to love your neighbor is strong. You shall love your neighbor and care for those who are experiencing difficulties. To be poor is not shameful; rather, it is a virtue. The weak and the meek on Earth are to stand far in front of the line at the gates of Saint Peter. Quite a few of us try to follow this message of love for our neighbors and respect for the weak. But beneath this layer of love for your neighbor, you'll find a little Norse troll, popping his head up and murmuring, *"Egi mått og mægin"; "Our own might and strength."* From the depths comes an uncomfortable disgust for those who cannot manage by themselves and an admiration for the strong. In Norse mythology, the warrior who died in battle was invited into Valhalla to eat at Odin's table. The strongest had the right to rule, and the world was no place for weaklings.

In person-oriented astrology, the planets are symbols for parts of the psyche. Mythology also gives us symbols for the inherent elements of the human psyche and the processes between their different parts. This means that every mythology will mirror the process that is going on in the psyche of the people who created it.

In this work, I have used astrology as a map that one can utilize to learn about and understand Norse myths. This led to a new and valuable insight into the planets' qualities and inherent relationships. Considering this connection, it is interesting to mention that Rudolf Steiner, "the father" of anthroposophy, said that a new view of cosmic connections would come through a new understanding of Norse mythology.[2] In the following chapters, I will show how Norse mythology can give a coherent and logical view of the world, which is just as marked by common sense and insight about cosmic laws as other belief systems.

I intend to show how these myths can be used to understand the horoscope and the processes we struggle with in our own lives. Norse mythology is not a useless and old-fashioned way of understanding ourselves and the universe; on the contrary, it is one of the most fascinating and involved topics one can learn about. We shall see how the Norse myths tell the story of the development of individual consciousness, history, and direction.

In Greek mythology, Uranus was overthrown by his son, Kronos (Saturn), who was, in turn, taken over by his own son, Zeus (Jupiter). In Norse mythology, the highest god of the heavens still sits in his high seat. He is filled to the brim with wisdom and insight, from which we can drink to our heart's desire. Odin is the protector of wizards, magicians, and soothsayers, just like the planet Uranus as a planet is primarily connected with astrology, other kinds of truth-seeking, and revelation of cosmic wisdom, and who is a better fit than astrologers to provide a serving of Odin's mead of wisdom?

I will begin with the creation of the world. I will then look at each of the gods and show the process of the Norse universe. It is in continuous motion toward Ragnarök—the end of the world. Everything in the world seems to be a natural consequence of having been formed. But do not despair, because when the Æsir and jötnar meet at the last great battle, and the world sinks into the sea, a new world is born, like the phoenix out of the ashes.

You are hereby invited to join on a voyage in your own unconscious and the old Norse world of the gods.

---

2   Rudolf Steiner, *Anthroposophical Leading Thoughts* (Rudolf Steiner Press, 1973).

In the Beginning Was Ginnungagap

Hear me, all in silence, hallowed beings
Both high and low Heimdall's children:
Thou wilt, Valfather, that I will tell
The fates as told from old which I recall.[3]

Ginnungagap is the abyss from which illusions rise. It is where nothingness has become and where everything is still possible.

In earliest times
Was not sea nor sand nor soothing waves,
Earth was not, nor upper heaven
But ginnunga gap and grass nowhere.[4]

Neither time nor distance is born, and in Ginnungagap, nothing can be measured. But on each side of the cosmic vagina of Ginnungagap, possibilities begin to grow out of the darkness. Two forces rise forth and take the form of two worlds. The unborn is in motion and divides itself in order to give birth to itself. On one side of Ginnungagap, a fire kingdom begins to take shape. There, all creative force of the universe is gathered, encapsulated like an egg in the depth of the cosmic belly of Muspelheim.

On the other side, an infinite world of ice rises forth. In Niflheim, layer upon layer of fertility is gathered, like blocks of ice. It curls itself together and waits to become. Niflheim is the lowest of the nine realms of death, nearest the place where the creations of Ginnungagap are to stream forth. Where nothing exists, the point out of which life is born.

Ginnungagap has become a cleft separating yin from yang, warmth from the chill. The unformed cosmos has made itself pregnant. The seed begins to form cracks, and in its longing to use the creative force, sparks fly from the fire world, jump over

---

3 Author translation of Snorri Sturluson's "Völuspá," *The Poetic Edda*.
4 Ibid.

Ginnungagap, and reach the ice waste, which slowly melts. Out of Ginnungagap's mother-bosom, Niflheim's ice begins to pour, thawed by the heat of the creative force.

Fertility streams out into the cosmos and begins to fill what was not with being. The brooks, called Éliváger, are the streams upon which time itself flows. Time is Ginnungagap's oldest child. A movement born out of illusions plays, and fertility and the created cosmos are born out of Time's life-giving waters. In the frosty smoke coming up from Ginnungagap's maternal womb, the cow, Audhumla, grows forth. She is love flowing out of the cosmic bosom. She feeds on the timestream and transforms the cold, newly-melted ice water into warm nourishment. In her, the heat of Muspelheim lives, too.

With endless patience, she works with the first whirls of dust, which are thrown around within the frame of time and space. Audhumla patiently licks salt off a large stone that grows up from the timestream as her soft tongue strokes across it. Out of this stone, the brilliant Búri grows, and he is given a son named Borr, who fathers the three brothers Odin, Vé, and Vili. They are the immanent divine consciousness of the universe who rose together with the work of creation.

Of the drops of ether that splash from the timestream, a jötunn (giant) grows forth. Dust particles collect in whirls. Slowly, matter begins to take shape. Aurgjelme is the name of the first jötunn, and from him, with a mighty speed, his stock spread throughout the universe.

Matter fills what was absent of being with being.

Neath the arms of the giant
Man and woman grew together
One of the feet
Begat with the other
A six-headed son.[5]

---

5   The author's translation of Snorri Sturluson's "Vavtrudnesmál," *The Poetic Edda*.

The jötnar (the race of giants) are the untamed energies of the universe, and they are Pluto. The jötnar are atoms dividing; one foot breeds with the other and produces a six-headed son. The original force of Pluto is turned out of the maternal lap. Here lies the untamable will to life and movement yet not conquered by consciousness.

Jötnar land, Jötunheimr, is where war happens. The jötnar are connected with the law, saying that what has become must be recreated, multiply, and perish. In Indian mythology, Kali, the terrible mother, represents this force.[6]

The jötnar are the mythological forces of chaos. They fight and tear down the ordered universe the gods try to build. At the same time, the jötnar often have wisdom and knowledge that is as great or greater than the Æsir. The jötnar, like Pluto, represent unavoidable destiny, structures that must disappear and end in chaos, regardless of how well-ordered the world is.

Audhumla is a force of love flowing out of Ginnungagap; the energies of the planet Neptune, as Audhumla, give love to all living things, including the jötnar. What else can she do? The jötnar are her children, born of her caring. As we shall see, the forces of Pluto and Neptune take on many forms as the Norse universe expands and unfolds—but Audhumla and the jötnar are the first forms these energies take after illusions start to pour out of Ginnungagap.

---

6 Wendy Doniger, "Kali." *Encyclopedia Britannica,* 13 Dec. 2023.

ODIN AND URANUS

Odin is the highest god of the heavens in Norse mythology, filling the same place as Uranus in Greek mythology. The northern Germanic name of Odin, *Wotan,* tells of one who travels with the wind. Consciousness and the element of Air are both the hallmarks of Uranus and Odin. These are only some of the vast similarities between the two figures. Odin is full of wisdom. Even if he is the highest god of the heavens, Odin is unconventional and unaccountable. He can emerge unexpectedly anywhere, and there are rumors in Asgard that Odin has disguised himself in women's clothing and exploring the vast realms of his sexuality.

The three outer planets, Pluto, Neptune, and Uranus, represent collective energies. Dane Rudhyar has called them the "ambassadors of the galaxy."[7] Of these, Uranus lies closest to Saturn and the physical reality. Uranus rotates "standing up." It always has one side pointed inward and one side pointed outward. From this, we can understand the myth of Odin's two eyes. One sits where it "should" and is turned toward the world of the humans,

---

7   Dane Rudhyar, *The Astrology of Transformation* (Theosophical Publishing House, 1980).

facing the Sun. The other lies a pawn for all the wisdom in the world, in the well of the ancient jötunn Mímir. This eye looks outward toward the Milky Way and the cosmic laws.

Odin (Uranus) thus becomes the one who mediates the cosmic laws of creation and the universe to humans. Odin knows the art of magic; that is, he knows the methods of manipulating the physical reality with words, consciousness, and understanding the laws of energy. Again, we find clear similarities to Uranus' intuitive influence on the horoscope. This way, Uranus becomes a point where we automatically know which laws actually count and what is happening at a deeper level. Odin, however, has one great grief. Despite all his wisdom and knowledge, he is still bound to the created universe and Ragnarök—the destruction of the world. In other words, he can understand and use the energies of the universe, but he cannot change them. The universe follows laws that even Odin must obey.

The name of Odin's throne is Hlidskjalf. From it, he can look out upon the whole world. It is tempting to think of Hlidskjalf as being the center of consciousness. In the physical body, Hlidskjalf corresponds with the pituitary gland. Odin is also accompanied by two ravens, *Huginn* and *Muninn,* "thought" and "memory." They are the antennas we so often connect with Uranus. The birds fly out into the world and tell Odin about all that which he has not had time to follow. The Uranus energy grasps everything that is happening, even if the mind is busy with other things. If it should later be necessary to retrieve any of what has happened in the deeper layers of the mind, similar to the contents of a tape-recording, all one must do is make contact with Huginn and Muninn.

TWO TYPES OF WISDOM

There are two types of wisdom in the created cosmos of Norse mythology. One is the consciousness of Odin, connected to Uranus and the element of Air. The other is the wisdom of the Völva and the Norns. They are connected to Pluto, Jötunheimr, and the primitive force. Another way of understanding this is the feminine force and wisdom in contrast to the masculine force.

As we shall see, the Norse gods are, first and foremost, men. It relates to a warrior mythology and is dominated by the values of men. On the other hand, the feminine exists like an underlying stream, consisting of enormous force, leading to developments just as important as the masculine. In many ways, we are witness to the struggle of consciousness and the individual to control the instincts and the primitive forces: the masculine effort to master the feminine. This had to end with Ragnarök.

Why, then, did this world develop? Could not Ginnungagap just as easily have kept itself closed forever?

THE SACRIFICE OF ODIN

One story tells of how Odin sacrificed himself by hanging upsidedown on the tree Yggdrasil for nine days and nights.

Yggdrasil is a symbol of the created world, and I will return to this later. But the name "Yggdrasil" comes from *Ygg*—another name for Odin, and *drasil,* which can mean a "pack horse" or "that which carries." Yggdrasil—the created world—is the horse that carries Odin.

> *I ween that I hung on the windy tree,*
> *Hung there for nights full nine;*
> *With the spear I was wounded, and offered I was*
> *To (Odin), myself to myself,*
> *On the tree that none may ever know*
> *What root beneath it runs from where the roots flow.*[8]

The divine consciousness is caught and suffers from having to be in a bound form. But through hanging on the Tree of the World, Odin got hold of runes and learned to make magic rhymes (galdr). In other words, he acquired wisdom.

This is reflected in Nordic mythology, where being becomes aware of its own existence and own potential through exploring the physical world. The created world is thereby the universe on the verge of discovering and unfolding its own possibilities. Again, we can return to Uranus to get an understanding of the longing for absolute freedom we find in this energy. The one eye looking out toward the cosmos sees the possibility of absolute freedom, whilst the eye looking in toward the Earth is bound and learns from the matter. It is painful to hang on the tree.

But Odin fell down and went out into the world to use what he had learned. The energy of Uranus must be used

---

8   The author's adapted translation from Henry Adams Bellows (trans.) and Snorri Sturluson, "Hávamál," *The Poetic Edda* (American-Scandanavian Foundation, 1923).

and tried out. As already mentioned, the world was created through the tension between two opposite poles: Niflheim and Muspelheim. These opposites are carried on to the struggle between the jötnar and the Æsir. The jötnar are the untamed forces of chaos in the universe, whilst the Æsir are the ordered forces trying to build a structured, ruleable, and comprehensive cosmos. The myths tell us how Odin and his two brothers, Vé and Vili, killed the gigantic jötunn Ymir. They used the giant's dead body as raw material to form the Earth and the heavens.

> *Out of Ymir's flesh was fashioned the earth,*
> *And the ocean out of his blood;*
> *Of his bones the hills, of his hair the trees,*
> *Of his skull the heavens high.*[9]

HUMAN BEING IS CREATED

Now, the world has been created, and the time is near for humans to tread into the arena. The myths tell of Odin and his two brothers and how they will one day walk along the beach where they find two tree trunks.

The trees are symbols of life energy. When examining a pack of tarot cards, we find rods representing the element of Fire. The Earth was created from Ymir's body, and the sea, the element of Water, had carried the tree trunks to the beach where the gods gave them life. Odin's gift was spirit and breath of life, the element of Air. We see how all the forces from the beginning of the world are gathered together in humankind, a micro-universe mirroring the great universe.

Until now, we have understood the myths as being stories about the creation of the world, the cosmic story, but with the creation of human beings, something new happens. The mythology no longer speaks of the outer universe alone. It

---

9   Henry Adams Bellows (trans.) and Snorri Sturluson, "Grimnismol," *The Poetic Edda* (American-Scandanavian Foundation, 1923).

describes every single individual's inner universe, which, of course, is a mirror reflection of the outer.

The human body came from the jötunn Ymir and is bound by the primitive forces, the forces of chaos that must perish. But consciousness comes from the Æsir and might have a chance of surviving even Ragnarök. The fight between the jötnar and the Æsir, when viewed in this way, becomes an ongoing struggle inside every one of us. Odin's brothers disappear from the saga more or less after humans were created. This can be understood in several ways.

1. They do not represent the Uranus energies—wisdom— that was available to humans.
2. The brothers represent energies that are gathered in Odin.
3. The brothers represent parts of the cosmic consciousness that, from now on, exists in the consciousness of humans.

As usual, it is impossible to be sure of anything when Uranus is concerned. Now, three mighty maidens arrived from Jötunheimr to confront humankind. They are the Norns: Urd, Skuld, and Verdandi—what was, what is, and what will be. Because humans are bound by the laws of the created world, the Norns spin a thread of destiny for each human being. Humanity is trapped by its fate, something called "karma" by those in the Eastern spiritual traditions. The created world must follow certain laws that all creatures must follow. To perish is a necessary consequence of what it is to be. Even Odin, with all his wisdom, cannot stop the world in its eternal motion: a motion stirring the ordered universe the gods want to build.

Here, we can receive a new key to understanding Uranus. This energy is connected with a search for freedom, but it also represents a need for order and structure, a system that guarantees freedom, equality, and fellowship for all. The order Uranus tries to establish is the ideal order, something that is very difficult as long as the jötnar and Pluto ensure that everything is perpetually moving. Remember the sign that Uranus rules, the Water-bearer, a fixed Air sign; he would rather solve all problems once and for all. In the same way as the Æsir and Odin, humanity is, regardless of their wisdom, subject to fate, the will of the Norns.

The transforming forces of Pluto ensure that nothing is static. The Norns are not mentioned to be goddesses of death but instead are goddesses of faith.

The Norse Cosmos

View of the World and Yggdrasil

One of the old worldviews was that the Earth was flat and that whoever sailed too far would disappear over the edge and fall down into nothing. This is a notion that has been reborn as a possibility by a group of people who seemingly spend a lot of time with virtual reality and, in some way, have reverted back to an understanding of a two-dimensional universe.

In the middle was Asgard, the home of the gods. All around was Midgard, the home of the humans, and outmost lay Jötunheimr and Utgard, where the jötnar and forces of chaos dwelt. If we regard this to be a picture of the psyche, we see that the center relates to Asgard—the spiritual, divine part of man. Asgard is the center of our soul. Surrounding us is what corresponds to Midgard, the world of humans, the area where spirit and form meet and the point where the world or society meets. Outside corresponds to Jötunheimr, the landscape of chaos and all that is threatening or enticing, the subconsciousness we have not yet conquered.

Yggdrasil

There is also another picture of the world in Norse mythology. As mentioned, Yggdrasil is described to be the created world, the world Odin rides. Yggdrasil is an ash tree, and in Nordic mythology, the first human beings were also created from this tree. In this way, we see how the tree stands as a symbol of the outer world where humankind lives, but at the same time, it is a picture of the individual human.

Yggdrasil has three roots. It sucks nourishment from three dimensions. From these three dimensions (width, length, and height), the fourth—matter—rises. A large worm gnaws at one of the roots. On the tree top, an eagle sits with a hawk between its eyes. We know the symbols form the sign of Scorpio: the snake that is transformed into an eagle.

Between the two, the squirrel Ratatosk flies with messages. The snake is symbolic of humanity's drives and impulses, but it also represents the kundalini energy lying there latent. The squirrel represents the nerve impulses, flying back and forth between instincts and consciousness, of thought trying to hold the various parts of the psyche together.

The eagle is the part of our instincts that has been transformed into a higher level. The hawk sitting between the eagle's eye represents our third eye. By opening up the third eye, a person becomes able to stand and look out on the limited world we usually call reality and see it as it really is. The eagle and the hawk sit at the top of the tree, so far up that they can look out at the whole landscape, the larger perspective that comes with a developed consciousness. Four stags gnawing at the top of the tree are the innocence and beauty that one finds at this level of consciousness. But, as mentioned before, the worm, representing our drives and impulses, is mercilessly ravaging one of the tree's roots.

In "Grímnismál" of *The Poetic Edda,* we can read about the sufferings of Yggdrasil:

> *The ash Yggdrasil meets a destiny*
> *Worse that no one can know*
> *A heart beats the top*
> *The trunk is rotting*
> *And at the bottom*
> *Nidhugg (Nithhogg) is gnawing.*[10]

---

10 The author's translation of Snorri Sturluson's "Grímnismál," *The Poetic Edda.*

The Well of Mímir and the Hrimthursar (frost giants) dwell under another root. From here comes the primal force that nourishes the tree. The tree is also overwhelmed with nourishment from above. It is mentioned as a white spiritual light or stream of energy that flows without ending upon the created world. At the second root is Hel, death, where the Norns—the goddesses of faith—also dwell. From here comes the force enabling the old to disappear.

In "Völuspá" from *The Poetic Edda,* it is told that by the third root, humankind dwells. Seen from this angle, humankind is caught between what is to be and what will perish.[11] Without an understanding of its own destiny, humanity is the worm Nithhogg, gnawing and ravaging at the third of Yggdrasil's roots. We can quite clearly see how the living Earth is moaning, turning, and shivering in the pain brought on by humanity's poisonous fangs. There is a legend about Odin where we again meet the motive of the snake and the eagle. It tells of how Odin became the god of the poets.

ODIN AND THE MEAD OF SUTTUNGR

Once, there had been a war between the Æsir and the Vanir, who were the gods of fertility.[12] When they made peace, they sealed the agreement by spitting in a vessel, among other things. From this spit, which represents pure essence, they made an exceedingly wise man named Kvasir. Kvasir was formed by divine energies, and the gods were the conscious forces of order in the universe. Kvasir is a symbol of direct contact with this essence.

The myth goes on to tell how Kvasir was murdered by two dwarfs who poured his blood into three vessels. The same dwarfs also killed a jötunn, but this jötunn had a brother,

11   Henry Adams Bellows (trans.) and Snorri Sturluson, "Voluspo," *The Poetic Edda* (American-Scandanavian Foundation, 1923).

12   Anthony Faulkes (ed.) and Snorri Sturluson, *Edda: Skáldskaparmál* (Viking Society For Northern Research, 1998).

Suttungr, who threatened to take their lives if he did not receive the three vessels. This is how the mead, held within those three vessels, came to Suttungr's hands when Odin went to Jötunheimr to fetch it. To go to Jötunheimr means to travel to an unknown and dangerous place, the parts of the psyche not yet known or explored.

When one tries to fetch something up from one's unconsciousness, it seldom helps to go for it head-on, so Odin first goes to Baugi, Suttungr's brother. This brother had nine bondsmen out in the field, cutting grass. Odin offered to sharpen their scythes. When this was done, their scythes were so sharp they cut the hay without any effort. Odin is the Uranian awareness, sharpening consciousness to its utmost capabilities.

The bondsmen wanted to buy the whetstone that Odin had used to sharpen their scythes. Odin threw it up into the air and said that he who caught the whetstone could have it. In their greed, the bondsmen cut each other's heads off while scrambling to catch the stone. Odin offered to serve instead of them and do nine men's work on the condition that Baugi would help him get a sip of Suttungr's mead when the work was done. Here, we see how consciousness must free itself from the bonds of slavery and follow the same laws the unconscious goes by when it wants to reach the poet's message, the creative art that rises from direct contact with the essence of existence, the gods' spittle.

When the time came for Odin to have his wage, Baugi went to his brother to retrieve it. However, when asked, Suttungr was not willing to give so much as a drop of his mead away. Steady and hard work is not enough to reach the deeper secrets of the unconscious. Odin now finds a drill and tells Baugi to make a hole through the mountain to where Gunnlöd, Suttungr's daughter, watches over the mead. Consciousness must be as sharp as the razor's edge and get help from the forces that lie in unconsciousness. In order to have the poet's mead, even Odin must be on guard. To wander in this unknown and unaccountable part of consciousness is always dangerous.

Baugi says the hole is ready, but when Odin blows into it, the filings of chipped rock fly back. This happens twice before Odin sees the filings fly through to the end of the hole. Immediately, he turns himself into a snake and writhes inside the hole. Baugi sticks the drill after him, but he is too late. Both cunning and wit are needed if one is to enter the center of the unconscious, where the divine essence is.

ODIN QUENCHES HIS THIRST

Gunnlöd, the daughter who guards the precious mead, is an anima figure. She represents the inner feminine part of Odin, and in order to have access to the mead, he has to sleep with her. He must surrender to the forces of his own unconscious and make them pregnant or let himself become pregnant by them. We recognize the motive from all the fairy tales about the troll who has captured the princess and locked her up in the mountain. We also recognize that an artist must become pregnant with creative energy to give birth to the inspired work of art.

This is the place where art is born. He stayed there for three nights and emptied one vessel of mead every morning. After having drunk all the mead, Odin turned himself into an eagle and flew away. We can see how Uranus in the horoscope represents a point where we have a possibility to enter our unconscious and have direct contact with the essence of the universe—all the wisdom and creative force in the world. At the same time, this voyage means a transformation from snake to eagle, from instinctive to having a superb overview. To enter this center, we must use and acknowledge our own instincts and pure energy, but in order to come out, this energy must be transformed into consciousness.

We recognize the picture of the worm gnawing at Yggdrasil's root. The Scorpio energy is transformed into the eagle at the treetop when it has risen to the center of consciousness. The hawk symbolizes the same thing as Suttungr's mead: the ability to open up to other senses and look into the essence of things.

But the task does not end there, for carrying Suttungr's mead can both be heavy and dangerous.

Our unconscious does not like to give anything away. When Suttungr hears about Odin's theft, he is furious and follows him with a terrible speed in his own eagle form. The trip back to consciousness with the experiences and the insights that have been brought up from our unconscious is not an easy task. When the other Æsir notice that Odin is on his way, they put vessels and bowls out so that Odin can empty the mead into them. The rest of the psyche stands ready to receive what Uranus has brought up from the unconscious.

But Suttungr is so close that Odin must free himself of some of the mead in order to avoid being caught. These drops remained on the ground so that anyone could help themselves to it. They are called "the rhymester's share" and symbolize bad and misunderstood art. Artists and mystics who have been too hasty or who have not been willing to do the necessary work that allows them to drink Suttungr's mead use these drops that were spilled by Odin from his rectum. We can find a connection between Suttungr's mead and Mímir's Well. Kvasir was so wise that he knew everything, which is preceicely what will become of whoever drinks from Mímir's Well. In "Völuspá," the Völva, or wise woman, says:

> *Mead is drunk by Mimir*
> *Every morning*
> *Out of Odin's pledge*
> *Do you know enough…or what…?*[13]

Odin, or Uranus, has not made this voyage through the unconscious untouched. His one eye lies as a pawn. When something must be paid, pawned, or suffers a misfortune in the myths, it is because it happens of necessity. To drink

---

13   The author's translation of Snorri Sturluson's "Völuspá," *The Poetic Edda.*

from Mímir's Well—Suttungr's mead—means that one eye is left behind. After this experience, the view of the world will never again be the same. From now on, the outer world is only half of reality. The other half remains on the other side of the illusion's veil.

ODIN IN VALHALLA

The Uranus-Odin figure seeks to bind two worlds together, to give words to what is unsaid, and to give form to what is without form. Odin's castle in Asgard is called Valhalla. All who die in battle go there. On a symbolic level, this means those who die in battle in order to live in harmony with the divine laws. Odin himself does not eat, for he only drinks wine. Wine is probably the closest humans have come to the inspiring mead of Suttungr. Odin does not need food because he represents spirit and consciousness.

In Valhalla, the Kingdom of Uranus, there is never a lack of anything. Odin knows that the source where everything comes from—Ginnungagap—is inexhaustible. But Odin, like Uranus, is no peaceful fellow. He brings struggle and unrest to the psyche. Only through struggle can the mind develop, learn, and prepare itself for the last big settlement—Ragnarök. Odin has a number of names in mythology, and he can appear in unexpected costumes and contexts. No one can be completely safe from Odin's ideas, but at the same time, he is wise and just. A behavior one absolutely can recognize where Uranus fares forth in the personal horoscope.

In Odin, we have a remarkable god. A god that created the world, not to be venerated or adored, but to use the world as a vehicle to gather wisdom. That is his first and, by far, biggest aim and interest. It tells a story where the gods created the universe to become aware of themselves, and humankind and human consciousness are part of this spirit of the gods or God exploring and discovering its own nature and true existence.

LOKI AND MERCURY

Loki is a very special character among the Nordic gods. I am not aware of any signs of him having been historically worshiped by human beings, yet he is still one of the most often mentioned in myths. Loki is Odin's foster brother, bound to him with a blood bond from the morning of time. This relation can be understood as the connection between Uranus and Mercury. Both planets are tied to consciousness and thoughts, but while Odin is bound to higher consciousness and understanding of fundamental and spiritual laws in the universe, Loki is associated with shrewdness, cunning, and logic.

Loki loves to play tricks and is not much concerned with morality, with right or wrong. We identify this with Mercury from astrology. When consciousness is seen from this perspective, it becomes an instrument used to handle and get to know the world around us. Just like Loki, consciousness, from this perspective, is a double-edged sword. There are more things connecting Loki to human beings. He is described to be the son of Laufey (meaning "leaf" or "foliage"). The green leaf-island is the Earth, floating through the cosmic sea. Both Loki and human beings are children of the Earth. He is, just like humans of mixed inheritance, with roots both among jötnar and Æsir. Therefore, the struggle between the forces of order and the forces of chaos in the universe is present in Loki.

Loki is, as we can see, a complex composition. He likes things to happen. Like Mercury and the concept of thought, he is constantly on the move and brings forth a combination of the most beautiful things and the greatest catastrophes. A special way of recognizing Loki is through his humor, something that also clearly separates him from the other gods. Loki is able to describe and experience the world as something absurd and contradictory. This is often one of the prerequisites of humor.

A JESTER AND A TRICKSTER

Once, the gods had to try to sweet-talk a violent jötunn woman named Skadi. One of her demands, in order to forgive the Æsir for the wrong they had done toward her, was that they should make her laugh. The jötunn woman symbolizes the feminine, sexual, primal force, and how can one amuse such a being? Well, by making the masculine sexual force seem ridiculous. We must remember that the Æsir were a masculine-domi-nated mythology, whilst the jötnar, by and large, were closely connected to the feminine force.

Loki takes a rope and binds one part of it onto the pride of his manhood. The other end, he ties to the beard of a billy goat. Loki and the goat scream and shout at each other as they pull and tug at the rope. Finally, the jötunn woman can no longer contain herself and breaks out into laughter. The masculine energy is made into a joke, unveiling its pity, and the jötunn woman is satisfied.

Loki has much of the trickster figure in him. He is sly and smart and never quite to be trusted. The Æsir must often press Loki with the worst threats in order to make him do what they want. In the same way, we can say Mercury and our thoughts often live lives of their own, independent of the rest of our personality. They have a way of going in their own direction and must often be coerced by our will and other parts of our psyche in order to do what is for our greater good.

Since Loki (and likewise Mercury) is not bound by the ancient primal laws, he is able to bring forth new and immeasurable treasures, but he is also the one who, in the end, brings about Ragnarök. I will explain later why this is a necessary consequence of Loki's existence. For now, know that he represents the limited reality which, out of necessity, must disappear in order for a new and more encompassing consciousness to rise forth. Meanwhile, however, the Æsir are dependent on Loki in order to fight the jötnar. He is the one who "tricks" the dwarfs into smithing the hammer of Thor, among other things.

One myth speaks of Loki cutting off Sif, Thor's (Jupiter) wife's hair.[14] The hair is a symbol of strength and power. To take the hair from Sif is to steal optimism and hope from the mind. This is something that our petty Mercurial thoughts have a tendency to do, considering how easily they see the world around us as meaningless. As a result, Thor became furious and threatened to take Loki's life if he did not amend the wrong-doing. Those parts of the psyche suffer when hope is absent and put thoughts to work in order to find new meaning.

---

14   Anthony Faulkes (ed.) and Snorri Sturluson, *Edda: Skáldskaparmál* (Viking Society For Northern Research, 1998).

LOKI AND THE CREATIVE FORCE

Loki's way out of this misery is to bring forth costly treasures by using his wit to create something new. He goes to some dwarfs, who promise to help him ease Thor's fury. The dwarfs are the forces and the riches lying deep in the Earth. Through cunning and wit, Loki makes them bring forth treasures that the gods cherish immensely. The powers that the dwarfs represent are connected with the energy of Taurus and the ability to create something from the forces of the Earth. It is not so strange that the dwarfs are well-willed toward Loki, for they work in the innermost of the same Earth from which Loki descends.

The dwarfs, named the Sons of Ivaldi, forge new hair of gold for Sif, and hope can be restored. At the same time, they built a ship called Skidbladnir and a spear called Gungnir. Odin is given this spear as a gift, as it is a magical spear that hits whatever he aims at. Odin throws it over the armies to give them either victory or defeat. A spear is the weapon with which the lower Mercurial consciousness meets the created world and makes it accessible to the higher intuitive consciousness.

Uranus-Odin's insight and understanding increase through Loki's experiences. In this way, the spear becomes a tool that the parts of our psyche in touch with the original cosmic laws (Uranus-Odin) can use in order to grasp physical reality. The spear is intuition and higher knowledge, cutting into the mist of folly and forgetfulness that often lies in the human mind.

But now Loki has gotten a taste for more. This was fun! What more can he make the dwarfs bring forth? This time, however, he must use cunning to make the dwarfs build costly things. He went to a dwarf and said, "I don't think your brother Sindri can forge gifts for the gods that can measure with what the Sons of Ivaldi have forged. He shall have my head if he can do so."

Loki's scheme means that he tried to squeeze more out of the earth than what comes naturally. We recognize the situation in the function of our own minds! Our thoughts and our consciousness (Loki's head) become captured by the dwarfs—the material consciousness—as the price paid to bring forth these treasures.

The dwarfs forge fantastic things from their raw materials, such as a golden-bristled hog named Gullinbursti that can run through air and across water faster than any horse on land. It lightens up, making night become the day when it appears. Fields and meadows rapidly grow where Gullinbursti goes forth. The hog is given to Frey, whilst Odin gets a golden ring called Draupnir, which drips eight new rings equally large to itself every night. Thor receives his legendary hammer, Mjölnir. It hits anything he throws it at and always comes back to Thor's hand like a boomerang. We see how Loki can be connected to the outgrowth of industry and culture. The hog Gullinbursti represents agriculture, developing technical tools for their use in this industry. At first, only picks and plows were used, but after a while, quite advanced machinery was invented. The field grows enormously and gives food to human beings, keeping away hunger and need.

Draupnir is connected to industry. Through using machines and technology, we can make things reproduce themselves, almost without our participation. Machines can run, and humans can rest. The hammer of Thor represents the weapons that our technology and industry can make. It is a tool to conquer the unknown and force the jötnar to their knees, enabling humans to "conquer" nature. But be warned, as the hammer always returns. We must taste the fruits of its use, and the laws of karma are built into this terrible weapon with such mighty force.

Loki's connection with the dwarfs is what gives us the possibility to use the resources of the Earth according to our own wishes so that we may either bless or destroy ourselves. As mentioned, Loki—and, by association, Mercury—is without morality. He does what is in his nature, namely, to use his wit to any end that suits him in the moment. Now, the other gods decide that these three items that Loki had the dwarfs create are valuable. The decisive item here is Thor's hammer, as, without it, the Æsir don't think they would have been able to fight off the forces of chaos (the jötnar).

Despite the bargain he made, Loki tried to buy free his head, but he could not run away this time. The dwarf Brokkr wanted his head, as promised. Loki fled, but Thor helped Brokkr catch him. A promise is a promise in Thor's eyes.

Then Loki, now after a pause of thought, said, "You have no right to possess the neck, and you cannot take the head without hurting it." Brokkr did not like this, but he had to confess that he was right—but at least he could sew together Loki's lips. And that is exactly what he did—Loki was later able to open his mouth again, but he forever had ugly scars from the sewing.

We here see how Loki, as well as the Mercurial consciousness, do not let themselves become tied down, neither by dwarfs and the laws of the Earth nor of the Æsir and the cosmic laws. Loki is and remains an independent busybody whose mouth is impossible to stop. He says what he wants. He curses in church and lies whenever it suits him.

But as we shall see, one of the things that happened before Ragnarök and the birth of the new Earth is that Loki's mouth actually was stopped. This can be understood on two levels. On one level, reason, along with our way of thought, is blocked so that it becomes impossible to find a way out of the misery. Or, as I choose to interpret it, thoughts must be quietened—by force, if necessary—for a new consciousness to grow forth.

The Brick Wall of Security

One day, a smith came to Asgard and offered to build a wall around the place.[15] The Æsir thought that such a protection against the jötnar could be a good thing to have, but when they heard the price, they had second thoughts. In exchange, the smith wanted the Sun, the Moon, and Freya herself. The gods turned down the offer until Loki came up with an idea. They could give the smith terms that were impossible to uphold!

---

15 Arthur Gilchrist Brodeur (trans.) and Snorri Sturluson, "Gylfagin-ning," *The Prose Edda* (American-Scandanavian Foundation, 1916).

The brick wall was to be ready on the first day of summer, and if it wasn't, the builder would have no right to his wages. The smith agreed to these terms as long as he was allowed to use his stallion, Svadilfari, to help him. This the Æsir found reasonable, and the smith proceeded.

Now, the work went on at an enormous speed, and the horse pulled stone blocks big as mountains in toward the wall, making it grow and grow. When three days were left before the first day of summer, the Æsir realized that the smith would accomplish his task, and they became deeply despaired. They did not know what to do, for without the Sun, the Moon, and Freya, the world of the gods and humans would soon lay dark and desolate. Eventually, they all went to Loki, who had tricked them into accepting the agreement and threatened to torment him most terribly if he did not use his wit to save them from this rut.

The brick wall represents security. In this context, the Æsir symbolize that part of the psyche wanting to be safe from unexpected attacks from the jötnar—symbolizing the unconscious. "Reason," in the form of Loki, persuades the psyche to go ahead with building a wall in defense against the forces of chaos, but what will happen if this wall is completed and security is achieved? Well, Freya, representing fertility, and the Sun and the Moon, representing the light of individual consciousness, will disappear. In other words, we can say that humanity is dependent on being in motion and changing in order to survive. The moment humankind becomes completely safe, and nothing new becomes of it, it will cease to exist. It becomes an empty shell, eventually disintegrating into nothingness.

Total security essentially means non-existence. Humanity is the arena where the struggle between the jötnar and the Æsir is played out. In a way, we need this wall to protect ourselves against going under into chaos. But if the margins become too tight, we cease to truly live within this security. And Loki, our thought, will suffer tremendously by sitting idle, locked up in such a meaningless, desolate safety.

THE SAVIOR MARE

One whole day goes by while Loki ponders how to get out of this rut. The smith works at night, but late in the evening, when the stallion is about to pull the stone blocks toward the wall, a mare appears from the woods nearby. The stallion becomes so wild and wanton that he pulls himself out of the harness and disappears into the woods with the mare. The smith becomes raving mad—he understands that the wall cannot be finished on time. To their great surprise, it is now revealed to the Æsir that it was a jötunn they were dealing with all along, and Thor beats this jötunn smith to death with his hammer.

The mare that appeared from the edge of the woods was none other than Loki in disguise. When thoughts have become entwined in a net of security and fears that they will not be able to get loose, only one option remains: to let instinct take the reins. The horses represent erotic force, a force that is almost impossible to bind to safety in the long run. The Æsir are shocked to discover that the smith was a jötunn in disguise. They thought that they were in control of the psyche by building this wall, the way that we feel we are in control by ensuring our security. The result of this restriction, however, would have been to let the forces of chaos take the upper hand, and this would have left the individual consciousness lying empty and devastated. It is the forces of chaos inside ourselves that want so much to build this wall of security around us, and the result will, in fact, be chaos.

It's important to mention once again that the world of the jötnar is absolutely necessary for the existence of the Æsir. The individual consciousness cannot exist without a connection with the collective unconscious and the personal unconscious; otherwise, there would be disastrous consequences.

Now, as for the two horses, they went about such business in the woods that you might expect from a mare and a stallion, resulting in Loki mothering a foal that was given the name Sleipnir. This horse was the fastest in the world and was given as a gift to Odin. Sleipnir stands for the force that is set forth by the meeting between reason and instinct. It is the "harnessed" erotic forces that our higher consciousness (Odin-Uranus) can use as a tool to reach those parts of the psyche it wishes to employ. Sleipnir runs just as well through the air as through water and on land. The energy he symbolizes can, in other words, go as easily through our feelings (Water) as our thoughts (Air) and as practical reality (Earth).

But Sleipnir is not Loki's only offspring. Together with a woman of the jötunn breed, he fathers three frightening creatures. The jötunn woman's name is Angrboda, which means "the one who gives warning of grief," and in truth, her children are hard to cope with. These three "adorable" children are Fenrir the wolf, Jörmungandr the Midgard worm, and Hel, the queen of the afterlife.

Loki's Offspring

Hel

Hel dwells in the realm of death. Half of her face is an icy blue, and the other is a pale white. Hel is connected to Pluto. Being the child of Loki, she is bound to see death as something coming out of the lower consciousness, a place of limited ability to understand the world's true meaning. Loki is the only one of the Æsir who believes that real death exists. Whilst the other Æsir know that nothing that is created can completely disappear, Loki (our Mercurial mind) believes this is possible. At the same time, Hel represents elements of the psyche that are displaced and famished, the deep parts of the psyche that don't get acknowledgment from the individual consciousness. That is why her table is named Hunger and her knife is named Starvation. The servants are lazy and are not up to anything.

On the level where we find Hel, almost all movement has ceased to exist. How can this be connected to the tremendous force of Pluto? Well, Hel represents abysses in the psyche that are so tremendous they can easily paralyze us when we come in contact with them. The displaced Pluto energy is laughing at us with its half-cadaverous face. At the same time, the face of Hel is a yin-yang symbol. By traveling through the underworld and meeting Hel, our fear of death, put into the world by Loki, is concerned. It is here, in the deepest parts of our consciousness, that the understanding of life's eternal movement lies.

Jörmungandr

The second child of Loki is Jörmungandr, Midgard's worm or the World Serpent. It grew so large that the Æsir threw it out into the oceans of the world surrounding Earth. It bites itself on its tail, and this is how it must lay until Ragnarök comes. Then, the mighty body turns itself up upon the Earth's crust in order to participate in the final struggle. The worm biting itself on its tail is an ancient symbol of eternity. It is also a symbol of energy.

On one level, one must see Jörmungandr as a ring of force, keeping the created world in place within time and space. It represents the border for how far out into the unknown gods and humans can go. On this level, Jörmungandr is a protector, but on another, it is the guard of the gate. It is the monster that keeps us locked in a limited reality. In fairy tales, the guard of the gate is always a mirror image of whoever comes to pass through it. The energy of the guard is created by the shadowy parts of the seeker; it is an image of our fear and other darkness within the self. This is also the case with Jörmungandr.

The reason why it grows to be so enormous is that it lives of human beings' suppressed feelings. In a "civilized" world governed by "reason" and logic (symbolized by Loki), there is much that cannot unfold freely. There is much energy bound up. On the individual level, Jörmungandr becomes the monster that is created by our own suppressed feelings. Being reasonable and "civilized," we cannot allow ourselves to follow all our emotional impulses. These suppressions are necessary to create an organized society where humans can develop their individuality. This is just one of the reasons why Jörmungandr seems so dangerous. If we kill it, Midgard, the ordered world of humans, will fall apart. That the worm is found in the ocean emphasizes that it is within the realm of emotions where it tumbles about.

Fenrir

The third of this threesome is Fenrir the wolf. Originally, the Æsir let the wolf go freely around them, but it feeds on all the injustice and suppressed rage in the world. As can be expected, it soon became so wild and unruly that the Æsir worried about what would become of it. The suppressed rage of the whole world can be quite explosive. Only Tyr, being the bravest of the Æsir, still dared to feed and be around this fearsome wolf.

Tyr is a mighty warrior god, representing a pure form of Mars, but was hardly mentioned in the Norse myths. In the time of the Vikings, Tyr was barely worshipped, and we have very few stories saved about him. It may seem strange that he is not more apparent in the warrior's world of the Vikings. This absence can be attributed to his representation of a way of acting out the force of Mars that is older than what is prevalent in Norse society. Another reason can be that the force of Mars was so important for the human consciousness of that time that all of the gods shared in its aspects. Both Odin and Thor had this warrior aspect as a part of their nature. That being said, we find the purest form of Mars energy in Tyr and, as I will discuss later, in Frey.

The principle Tyr has for the law is fairly simple. If two people disagreed, they formed a circle and fought using single arms, and the winner of the fight was the victor. In other words, the word of the strongest is the law. As mentioned, the society where the Vikings came from was already arranged by other principles. Loki, the thought of reason, had started to put tight restrictions on the kind of enfoldment of Mars energy represented by Tyr. Tyr is not known to be one who brings peace. Being bound to the old rules means that he represents organized battle, not from behind and with shady methods, but open, fair, and honest in war or at single arms.

It is not hard to see that traces of this experience of Mars energy are still stored in our psyche. Phenomenons such as Naziism and despise for the weak are connected to abundant admiration of the use of power to do whatever one feels is right. The only surviving myth about Tyr is connected to the wolf Fenrir and makes the pieces fall in place in such a way that the puzzle almost solves itself. Tyr, as we know, represents the original use of Mars energy, whilst Fenrir is the animal groaning in us when we no longer can let it freely unfold.

The myth tells of how the wolf grew so incredibly large and wild that the Æsir became frightened of letting it loose upon the world; therefore, as an act of protection for all, the wolf force is leashed. The Æsir decided to have the wolf bound by a giant chain that Odin instructed the dwarfs to weld. Tricking Fenrir to wear it, the Æsir presented it to the wolf and asked him to show his might by trying to break it. Fenrir let them bind him in the chain; he was confident about his ability to easily escape. Fenrir's confidence was correct, as using his great strength was enough to stretch the chain a little, and then it went asunder. His awesome rage was not easily put in reigns.

The Æsir did not give up that easily. They had a new chain made that was twice as big as the first. They told the wolf that he would become very renowned for his might were he to break apart such a masterly piece of the smith's work. They saw that the chain was strong, but his strength was also great, and it continued to grow. He let the Æsir bind him, put his feet on the ground, and pulled so that the chain broke and flew in all directions.

Now, the Æsir were really afraid that the wolf would become so mighty that they would be unable to control him. Odin understood that there was no way to stop the rage and the mighty Mars energy by force. Here, one had to go by hook or by crook. He made the dwarfs weld a very special chain. It was made of a collection of peculiar ingredients: the roots of the mountains, the sinews of a bear, the beard of a woman, the sound of cats' feet, the breath of fish, and the spit of a bird. This chain represents the forces of nature tamed and bound in the human consciousness, which is, therefore, not found in nature as it is experienced by human consciousness. In order to control the wolf, the experience of reality first had to be cut down. The new leash was made smooth and soft like a band of silk.

When the Æsir came along with it and asked the Fenrir to try to tear this thin band, he sensed something fishy. It had to be some kind of trick that they wanted him to break such a tiny and hardly noticeable chain; neither could he see any possible fame in it. But Fenrir was proud of his strength and liked to show it off, so eventually, he agreed to be tied up—on one condition. One of the Æsir had to lay their hand in his mouth. This would be used as an assurance that the Æsir were to keep their promise and release him from the chain in case it should reveal itself to be a scam and betrayal and be impossible to escape. For a moment, the Æsir became irresolute. They all knew they would not loosen the chain, and no one wanted to lose a hand. Eventually, the fearless Tyr went up and put his hand in the wolf's jaws.

At this, the wolf let himself be bound by the leash, and however much he pulled and tugged, he was unable to come loose. This chain was not hard, and didn't resist like the others had. Instead, it formed itself along the wolf's fur, followed along when he tightened his muscles and was always an exact fit to whatever he did. In this way, his fury was bound because it was no longer possible to fight any enemies. Eventually, the wolf gave in and asked the Æsir to loosen it. But then all the gods laughed—all except Tyr. When Fenrir realized the Æsir would not loosen the chain, he bit off Tyr's right hand.

Tyr, the old warrior god representing the right of the mightiest, was now mutilated. And Fenrir, symbolic of our psyches' tremendous primal force, was bound. In the civilized and ordered society, these raw and untamed forces had been tamed. Far down in the earth, in the subconscious, they rapidly tethered the leash, keeping it in check. The wolf tried to gnaw through the leash, but then, the Æsir thrust a sword into his mouth. Fenrir howled in pain, and froth bubbled from his mouth, but he could not free himself from the leash. The pain felt by being rendered unable to use his primal forces was inevitable.

The sword is an ancient symbol for the element of Air (as in the suit of the tarot card). Air represents thought, which is what we use to analyze the world. On a symbolic level, the sword is the weapon of the spiritual warrior used to cut through the illusions of reality. In the wolf's jaws, it's meant to be the senses of reason and logic that stop us from letting the enormous forces, symbolized by Fenrir, loose.

We see how the wolf, Loki's son, is given an unkind destiny. In order for human society and the individual consciousness and spirit to develop, these forces must be bound and reined. In this way, the wolf must stand bound until Ragnarök comes and all the forces in the cosmos gather for a meeting and a battle on a vast plain.

THOR AND JUPITER

Thor is the son of Odin and Jörd. He is consciousness and strength born out of the meeting between the heavenly god—the cosmic consciousness—and matter, Earth. The consciousness human beings bear is also made out of this meeting. Thor, therefore, carries with him a special meaning for the development of human society and the human consciousness. In the Greek myths, the heavenly god Uranus was "dismissed" by his son Kronos (Saturn), who was castrated and removed by his son Zeus (Jupiter).

In the Norse myth, the original god of the heavens kept his place at the top of the throne. We can say that the Norse myth has preserved an ancient understanding of the universe. It sees reality from an angle where cosmic wisdom is still in the center. Zeus and Thor, who represent Jupiter, are far more bound to humanity's daily life and its struggle to survive and expand its limited understanding of reality. In the Norse myth, we meet an insight that stems from a direct and intuitive understanding of cosmic laws. One question I've often met is whether those who worshipped the ancient Norse gods, those who kept these myths alive, knew what great understanding and depth hid behind these apparently simple stories. The answer to this, I do not know.

Maybe they understood this intuitively rather than on an intellectual level—which is what we often mean when we talk of understanding. What is most probable is that there were those who had a more or less deep knowledge of what the symbolic language really meant, whilst ordinary people had a more direct and prosaic relationship with the gods. The distinction between those who worshipped Odin and those who kept to Thor also tells us something about this. The earls (the upper class), soothsayers, mystics, and magicians kept to Odin, while ordinary peasants and servants were most enthusiastic about Thor. It was Thor who had the most holy sites and was by far the most popular god of his time—until Christianity took over. This is easily shown by all the places named after Thor (also spelled "Tor"), such as Torslanda, Torsø, Torshov, etc. Also, nowadays, Thor is very much used as a part of names, both for men and women.

THOR AGAINST ODIN

But also in Norse mythology, we find signs of conflicts between Thor and his father, Odin. There is a story where Thor wants a ferryman to take him across a river, and this ferryman is no one less than Odin himself in disguise. The river represents the border upon how far one can go with Jupiter's power. Large parts of the world and the psyche can be conquered and understood based on the energies of Jupiter (Thor). But there are areas where Uranus, intuition, and a deeper insight into cosmic laws are necessary to help us across.

The ferryman and Thor get into what can be called a "bragging competition." Thor gives an account of all his great pieces of work. How he, with might and strength, has killed jötnar and defended the world of human beings. The ferryman answers with strange stories about mystical women he has played with and outwitted. How he, through wizardry and magic, has formed his masterpieces.

He teases Thor and tells him that his wife has a lover at home. As we later shall see, this lover is no one less than Loki. That things don't go so well at home when Thor is out ravaging is shown time and time again. Here, we see how Jupiter (Thor) focuses on conquering the new, going into the unknown, whilst all that he already has conquered lies open and unprotected.

The ferryman also says the following:

> *In Val-land was I and waged battles*
> *Urged the nobles to fight*
> *Nor ever made peace*
> *Odin get earls*
> *Slain in the battles*
> *But Tor (Thor), the breed of thralls.*[16]

---

16   The author's translation of Snorri Sturluson's "Harbarthsljoth," *The Poetic Edda.*

The Vikings were very much occupied with where one ends up after death. In many ways, the best ending was to come to the halls of Odin, the afterlife of warriors. Ordinary people who worshipped Thor to protect their country, their properties, and their lives against unhappiness and misery came, of course, to Thor after their death. It was primarily he who protected the human world against the jötnar and helped them expand their territory. The ferryman's despicable statement must be understood to mean that those who worshipped Thor were the humans who were enslaved by their well-being and prosperity, those who sought a safe and comfortable life. According to the ferryman, however, those who were warriors and who loved and lived for the struggle in and of itself came to Odin.

Again, we can see the difference between Jupiter and Uranus. Those who are connected to Thor's Jupiter energy are primarily engaged in seeking a good result and reward. Those who put their bet on Odin's Uranus energies look upon action and the processes of our behavior as being the most important. War for the sake of war. On a symbolic level, spiritual development is for the sake of spiritual development.

Now, it can be difficult to connect the warlike and unseemly Thor to safety, growth, and prosperity. But it is just this tremendous use of Jupiter energy that Thor represents and which gives the opportunity to protect oneself against unrest and unpleasantness. Through surviving that which is threatening, peace is ensured. In traditional astrology, Jupiter is usually bound to pleasurable comfort, exaggerations, and delights streaming in without having to work one's wits off: optimism and an easy look at life. Here, it is important to understand that Norse mythology has grown out of a totally different climate. In the cold North, where winter and snow rule through great parts of the year, there is no sense in lying in your hammock, lazing about. Our whole culture is marked by an active use of Jupiter energy.

The world must be concerned. By and large, Thor gives us a picture of Jupiter energy as something we must use to fight with. Here lie possibilities, but they don't come without hard work. They must be won through battle and action. Of all the Northern European peoples' spirits, the Danish have perhaps the most in common with the Greek experience of Jupiter energy. This is reflected in a landscape that is far milder and less harsh than what we find in the other Nordic countries. Based on this knowledge, it then becomes easy to understand that Odin and the Vanir, another race of gods, were the most popular in Denmark, whilst Thor topped the list in Norway.

Thor is known for his outrageous temper. When he gets angry, he grows to enormous proportions. He loves good food and never says no to a barrel of mead—or eight. It comes as no surprise that Thor has problems controlling his pleasure in food, temperament, and drink. Avoiding exaggerations and ending before it's too late is a very real problem when it comes to Jupiter energy. To call Thor a rumbling boaster would not be completely wrong—he is grossly strong, and it is he the Æsir must trust when they are seriously threatened. The optimism of Thor, his strength, and his unstoppable faith in himself are frequently necessary to put the struggle against the forces of chaos in order. Thor's red hair fits well with Jupiter's ruling sign of Sagittarius. The naive self-confidence and openness toward everything, such as what we find in these energies, is often half the secret of being a winner in strife against darkness and forces of chaos.

Thor gives us faith in ourselves and provides contact with our own force and strength. Without that faith, we would not have much with which to fight against the jötnar. Thor has his limitations, as previously mentioned, even though he does not know them himself. He is often figured as a brutish bully, rather using his fists than his head. But in *The Poetic Edda's*

"Alvíssmál," Thor uses cunning and wit to conquer a dwarf. As it appears, Thor has a good head and thorough knowledge of cosmic history. Regardless of this ability, it would seem that he would rather experience exciting adventures and violent fights instead of using his wit.

THE DEFENDER OF GOOD

While Odin is of many minds and can see how all forces must be kept in balance so that the cosmos can be maintained, Thor has a one-track mind. He fights for the Æsir against the jötnar for the light and against darkness. Thor is unable to understand the necessity of the jötnar and the forces of chaos the way Odin does. If he began to have sympathy and understanding for the jötnar, then he would not be able to fight them as ruthlessly and effectively. Thor's world is divided between good and evil, right and wrong. A dangerous side of Thor's energy is our belief that we, with our human science, technology, and understanding, can conquer nature and the forces of chaos. It is a mistake that we think our own motives are all light, good, and well-meaning, whilst others' motives are evil.

We must realize that the jötnar are caricatures of Thor's strength. The fight between Thor and the jötnar is the struggle in ourselves: our shadow parts and destructive motives versus our ideals, visions, and beliefs for a better world. Thor's most important weapon is the hammer Mjölnir, corresponding to the thunder rod of Zeus. In Indian mythology, the god Indra has a thunder rod he uses in his fight against the dragon Vritra. Thor's main enemy in the fight against chaos forces is Jörmungandr, who represents feelings that are held back.

In true Jovian fashion, Thor will let loose all forces toward growth and prosperity, whilst Jörmungandr represents the opposite: what is held back, what binds the world together. Jörmungandr is also the border Thor cannot cross. The border of the ordered universe.

THE SLINGER OF LIGHTNING

Without hesitation, Thor uses his hammer to smash jötunn heads. It always hits what it aims at, and working like a boomerang, it returns faithfully to Thor's hand after every throw. In the Viking days, it was quite common to make jewelry in the shape of Mjölnir, a token used to protect humans against evil.

The image of the hammer returning to Thor's hand after every throw relates to the concept of karma: everything that Jupiter energy serves will eventually return to us once again. It renews itself all the time; optimism is never used up but returns again and again. This is also true, however, for the consequences of those actions put into life by our need to conquer and our optimism.

In our consciousness, Thor represents the philosopher, ever fighting for the individual to conquer new areas of the psyche. Thor travels through the heavenly vault with his two rams. He makes thunder (the word *thunder* is, in fact, derived from the name *Thor*) and lightning. By traveling through the air in myths and legends, Thor is symbolically connected to consciousness and mental processes: he represents mental discharges. When the cold and warm air streams meet, when contradictions in the psyche or consciousness and unconsciousness crash together, it is Thor in action, creating "Thor-weather," or thunder. It is he who cleanses the air, he who goes into the struggle and dissolves all the tension that has built up. He lets the wind and the rain sweep away all that is clammy and shut in so that the horizon can open again and let new light in.

One of Thor's names is Lynslyngeren (the Lightning Slinger). Jupiter and Sagittarius are connected to lightning—Fire in the Air. They are also connected to the color blue—the element of Air in the flame. A good exercise to help one to get better contact with these energies is to meditate upon the blue part of the flame of a lighted candle.

But this philosophy, which is connected to the individual consciousness, has its limit. It needs an ordered universe with which to organize itself. At the same time, it is constantly fighting to expand the very borders it operates within. Jörmungandr and Thor need each other in order to exist, but they are in a continual fight and kill each other in the end, at Ragnarök.

Thor can be understood as those energies that begin processes, those that are absolutely necessary at the early stages of an action's conception but that disappear once the target is reached. Among the Æsir, he is not alone in having such a function. Many of the gods do not return after Ragnarök but instead come home as their own sons and daughters, reborn aspects of the same energy.

THOR IN HYMIR'S FARM

Once, Thor visited the jötunn Hymir to fetch an enormous pot to be used for a feast the Æsir were planning.[17] Hymir lives east of Élivágar, beyond the timestream. Hymir is not a jötunn manifested in the real world. He is the actual essence of the untamed forces in the psyche that are impossible to get rid of, the very forces that have the great pot needed by the Æsir. Without it, they would be unable to brew enough mead to get them all ecstatically drunk. But here, east of Élivágar, they are also quite near the place where Jörmungandr stays.

Despite the danger, Thor rows ahead, and Hymir fishes a couple of whales. Thor, using the head of Hymir's best ox as bait, gets Jörmungandr on his hook. He pulls it to the side of the boat and hits it.

> *The monsters roared, and the rocks resounded,*
> *And all the earth so old was shaken;*
> *Then sank the fish in the sea forthwith.*[18]

---

17   Henry Adams Bellows (trans.) and Snorri Sturluson, "Hymiskvitha," *The Poetic Edda* (American-Scandanavian Foundation, 1923).

18   Ibid.

The earth shook. It would disintegrate if Jörmungandr disappeared. In his eagerness to prove his strength and conquer new land, we can see how Thor made the whole ordered cosmos creak at its joints. As mentioned previously, he had difficulties understanding that forces such as Jörmungandr are necessary for the maintenance of the universe, where the human consciousness goes through its process of development.

Regardless, the story naturally ends with Thor taking the pot from Hymir's farm. The jötnar searched for Thor, but they were no match against his strength. Using his hammer, he kills the whole bunch. The lay poem ends by explaining that now the Æsir are to make such a feast every winter and will use the vast pot brought to them by mighty Thor.

Here, we see how the pot represents the possibility of brewing oneself into a state of ecstasy. It represents the ability to make a ritual where the Æsir, the ordered part of consciousness, can give itself over to the ecstatic feeling of oneness with unconsciousness in safe and controlled forms. It has conquered the pot and can brew an appropriate portion of the mystical feeling of oneness on its own ground without risking attack or being sucked in by the jötnar, the chaos. The Jupiter energy in the horoscope gives us an opportunity to experience a controlled and limited unity with the universe. It provides a limited portion of ecstasy, but since it all happens on the individual consciousness' terms, it must only be a taste, a time-limited ritual.

Thor is, in other words, the Æsir's warrior put forth in the struggle against the jötnar and the forces of chaos that threaten the ordered world. He seeks to extinguish all trolls and demons in the psyche so that the individual consciousness can gain control and live in freedom and prosperity. It is worth mentioning that this safety is not achieved, however, because Thor tries to avoid difficulties and unpleasantness. On the contrary, peace is a result of him seeking and attacking the problems before they grow to be invincible. Thor's strength and courage ensure that the jötnar are unable to defeat the Æsir. He protects the individual consciousness from being extinguished by the tremendous and unruly forces of the unconscious.

Alas, Thor does not manage to conquer the jötnar entirely and get control of their world. He can go to Jötunheimr, the individual consciousness traveling in the unconsciousness or the collective consciousness, but in this landscape, he must follow the rules, and therefore, he often has his shortcomings.

We also hear of the jötnar who enter behind the wall of Asgard being granted a small chance of getting away in one piece. Parts of the collective psyche that, in one way or another, are integrated into the individual consciousness cease to be a part of the vast and threatening chaos and become instead a part of the ordered cosmos.

We see this exchange of energy between the jötnar and Æsir all the time. The Æsir marry and have myriads of children with jötunn women. We can see this as a symbol of the individual consciousness' attempt to conquer and impregnate the collective potential found in the psyche. This can be related to the story of Odin laying with Suttungr's daughter to get ahold of the mead. Likewise, the jötnar constantly sought control of the Æsir's women so that their world should not lay barren and unfertile.

THE LAY OF THRYM

A humoristic myth by the name of "Trymskvadet" or "Thrymskvitha" tells of how the jötunn Thrym had stolen Thor's hammer from him whilst he was asleep.[19] The only thing that would make Thrym give the hammer back was that the Æsir should give him Freya—the fertility goddess—as his bride. In the lay, it is mentioned that Thrym, the goblin king, buried the hammer eight leagues under the earth.

It is natural to think that the jötnar are not able to use Thor's hammer. This weapon, being connected to the light of

---

19   Henry Adams Bellows (trans.) and Snorri Sturluson, "Thrymskvitha," *The Poetic Edda* (American-Scandanavian Foundation, 1923).

consciousness, hope, technique, and direction, is unable to use the shadier shapes of the subconscious. They can, however, hinder consciousness from taking hold of its own strength.

That the hammer was stolen from Thor whilst he slept is also important. In the realm of sleep and dreams, it is the subconsciousness that takes control. But from this, Thor awakens and finds he is helpless. He tells Loki of this—the thinking ability—in order to get advice. Loki borrows the feathered cloak of Freya to enable him to travel down into the subconscious. He arrives at Thrym's farm and is told that Thrym has the hammer and will only give it back in exchange for Freya herself. They try to talk Freya into giving herself to Thrym, but she refuses.

When something happens in the myth, it is mentioned because, by necessity, it must happen that way. Freya refuses because she cannot marry Thrym. The jötunn represents a primitive level in the psyche that humans contact in order to regain their force and strength. In times of peace, Thor slept and lost the shrewdness that was necessary to fight against the forces of chaos. But Freya—Venus—has developed ideals and needs, making it impossible for her to accept life together with Thrym—the king of the goblins.

The Æsir are desperate to retrieve Thor's mighty hammer and gather to form a plan. The individual consciousness seeks everywhere to find a way to defeat the new threat. How is the courage and the strength necessary in the fight against the forces of chaos to be found? Finally, Heimdall, the wisest of the Vanir, takes the stand. He is connected to Saturn, and, as such, he is the one who represents the maintenance of the manifested and organized human world. Heimdall's proposition is that Thor must dress to look like Freya. This means that the masculine force of expansion must contact the feminine side of itself to regain its strength.

Initially, Thor refuses, unwilling to sacrifice his masculinity, even for a moment. What would the others think of him if he were to dress in women's clothes? But eventually, Loki manages to convince Thor. It is the only way to get the hammer back. And without the hammer, consciousness soon will be outweighed by an infinite stream of jötnar. The individual consciousness cannot stop its expansion. It exists as the force of a process where it continually seeks to expand its understanding and influence. If the process stops for even an instant, it will immediately reverse.

In the Lay of Thrym, we examine individual consciousness coming to a point where the masculine and feminine must begin to acknowledge one another within the self. Men must begin to connect with their femininity and women with their masculine energy. If they do not, consciousness and society will go under in a helpless, one-track mind without finding the hammer of Thor lying buried eight leagues under the earth, deep down in the collective subconsciousness.

THOR'S WEDDINGFARE

Eventually, acknowledging the gravity of the situation, Thor is persuaded to wear women's clothes. Loki, being more used to his feminity—and one who enjoys these kinds of tricks—comes along dressed as a servant girl. Loki has no morals, as earlier mentioned, and is not so worried about what others might think. We can imagine how this story has had a kind of redeeming and purifying effect when told. Through hearing how the mighty Thor had to dress up as a woman, the Vikings were likely given perspective and witnessed the irony of their own male ideals. In this way, they would have allowed themselves to bring out some more of their own sensitivity.

In anticipation of Freya's supposed arrival, Thrym throws a grand feast in Jötunheimr. Thor, dressed as Freya, eats and drinks heartily. He eats an entire ox and eight salmon, washed down with three full barrels of mead. We clearly recognize Jupiter's inability to know when to stop. This appetite gives the jötnar a scare as they start to ponder whether there may be a trick in the presence of Thrym's new bride. Despite the suspicion, Loki manages to calm Thrym by telling him that

Freya neither ate nor slept for eight nights because of her tremendous longing for Jötunheimr.

The feast ends with the wedding procession of Thrym to "Freya." As a wedding gift, Thrym places the hammer in the lap of his new bride. Thor sheds his disguise and immediately beats every jötunn, goblin, or troll around him to death. Through making contact with his feminine side, consciousness also has made contact with the primal forces represented by the jötnar in the psyche. Through this contact with the instinctive parts of the psyche, the individual consciousness re-conquers its strength and might, enabling it to defend and maintain its own existence. Here, we see a clear example of the interaction between the jötnar and the Æsir—between individual and collective consciousness.

The Æsir—individual consciousness—must defend their territory against the collective forces. But to achieve this, they have to use the energies available in the deeper layers of the psyche. Æsir and jötnar fight against each other, but the one cannot exist without the other. In the struggle between light and darkness, neither can ever win. But as we shall see later, there is a possibility that the struggle can develop into a point where the various parts of the psyche attain a higher realm of unity.

THOR AND UTGARD-LOKI

One of the most famous myths about Thor recounts the time he was invited to the home of the jötunn Utgard-Loki.[20] Utgard-Loki stands as a symbol for the logic of the subconscious and understanding of reality, in contrast to Loki, who represents individual consciousness, logic, and rational thinking ability. As we shall see, the subconscious plays tricks on and distorts our minds when it meets the conscious. In the subconscious, the world of symbols is reality.

---

20   Arthur Gilchrist Brodeur (trans.) and Snorri Sturluson, "Gylfagin-ning," *The Prose Edda* (American-Scandanavian Foundation, 1916).

One day, Thor was traveling with Loki and a servant boy called Thjalfe. We see that Loki and Thor once again travel together to Jötunheimr. The two do not make a bad team at all: Loki, with his cleverness and quick thinking, and Thor, with his strength, fearlessness, and courage. Loki—Mercury—can be very good to have at your side when you are traveling through Jötunheimr's dangerous landscape.

When evening fell, they found themselves in a large forest. Fortunately, they discovered a large house, which they entered. In this building, there was a large side room, and there they lay down to sleep. That night, a terrible storm began that caused the earth to tremble and shake. When morning came, Thor went outside and spotted a huge man sleeping and snoring. It wasn't a storm at all, but rather this giant's breath that had created the violent trembling. The house they had stayed in turned out to be a mitten belonging to this giant. The side room was the thumb. The individual consciousness can be confronted with quite overwhelming issues when it sets out on a journey in the unknown chaos of the subconscious.

Once the giant awoke, he joined the crew and kept them company on the road. They walked all day, and when evening arrived, the giant immediately prepared himself for sleep. Before he started to snore, he told his traveling companions that they were free to feed themselves from his food bag. There was just one problem: Thor wasn't able to unstring the satchel. He couldn't untie a single knot! Enraged, he took his hammer and slammed it against the giant's head. In response to mighty Thor's assault, the giant simply awoke and asked if it was an acorn that fell on him. Insulted, Thor became even more furious and struck again and again—but to no use. The hammer, which otherwise crushed everything in its path, seemed useless against this giant.

We remember how Odin used cunning on his journey in the subconscious. He knew the symbolic language that was necessary to understand this part of the journey and how to draw out one's secrets. Thor tries to find a solution head-on with courage, determination, and strength, but in this situation, such an angle is useless. When morning came, the giant awoke and said that they were close to Utgard-Loki's farm.

"Perhaps you will go there and try your luck," the giant suggested, "but you should probably turn around and go the other way. There is little to be gained for petty people like Thor in Utgard-Loki's halls."

Of course, this was the fastest way to irritate Thor, who would never back down from any superior force. Without hesitation, he marched straight into Utgard-Loki's halls. When they arrived, nobody noticed them, but eventually, Utgard-Loki took the time to speak to his new guests. He seemed amazed that this small man could be the Æsir Thor and wondered what kind of sports the visitors were good at. Only those more skilled than others in one area or another were allowed in his halls.

CONTESTS WITH COMPLICATIONS

Loki chose the eating contest as a competition. He believed that no one could eat faster than him. A tray of food was brought forward. Loki sat at one end, while a man named Logi (meaning "Flame") sat at the other. They started to eat with furious speed and met in the middle. Logi had eaten both the trough and its contents, while Loki had only eaten what was inside. It was clear to everyone that Loki had lost that contest. Thjalfe, Thor's apprentice, wanted to try his hand at racing. Utgard-Loki brought in a man called Hugi and cleared a good running track for the competition. Unfortunately, things did not go better with Thjalfe than they did with Loki. They tried three times, but Thjalfe only got further and further behind each time.

Then, it was Thor's turn to compete. He offered to have a drinking competition with someone. Utgard-Loki thought that sounded reasonable and went into the guild hall to get his drinking horn. He offered it to Thor and said that it is considered well drunk when the horn is emptied in one gulp—some empty it in two, but no one is so challenged that they can't even empty it in three gulps. Thor put his fortune on it and drank and drank.

Finally, he had to stop to take a breath, only to find that none of his guzzling had diminished the amount of mead in the horn. Furiously, he proceeded to drink once more, but it didn't help at all. Now, Thor was really getting angry. He put his lips to the edge of the horn and drank as deeply as he could. When he finally stopped, gasping for air, he saw that the contents of the horn had sunk ever so slightly. Utgard-Loki seemed disappointed that Thor did not have greater powers than that and wondered if he would rather try something else. He could, for example, try to lift the cat that was walking around on the floor.

"It's something the young men who live in the hall tend to have fun with," said Utgard-Loki.

Thor grabbed hold of the cat, which stretched its arched back as he reached to lift it into the air. Thor pulled with all his strength, but even so, he could barely lift a single one of the cat's paws. Utgard-Loki mocked Thor, who was now furious and desperate. Frustrated, he wanted to wrestle with someone to show his strength. Utgard-Loki thought that the men of his hall would find it disgraceful to wrestle with someone as tiny as Thor, but if he wanted to, he could try his hand at a little fight with Utgard-Loki's old foster mother, Elli.

The two gave in to wrestling, but the harder Thor tried, the firmer the old woman stood. As it was, she began using tricks, and Thor began to falter. Finally, he was forced to put one knee on the ground for support. Utgard-Loki interrupted the fight and said that it was evening and time for supper. They were served, shown to their bedchambers, and well-treated for the rest of their visit.

The individual consciousness becomes rather small when compared to the enormous forces that exist in the collective psyche, but it is still a great threat to the entire balance that maintains the cosmos. It shows that it is not only the individual psyche that must defend itself against attacks from the forces of chaos. The jötnar, the subconscious, must also protect themselves against the violent and purposeful force of the individual psyche so as not to be crushed and abused. The jötnar protect themselves here by using other dimensions of reality.

THE TRUTH COMES OUT

When they were about to say goodbye the next morning, Utgard-Loki followed them outside the gate and told them that it had all been nothing but deception and trickery. Had he known how strong Thor was, then he would never have let him into his castle at all. It was Utgard-Loki himself whom they had met in the forest. He had tied the food bag with troll iron, and three vast valleys erupted after Thor hit him with the hammer. They could see for themselves the three cliffs on the horizon, each of which had its own valley where the hammer had hit, with one deeper than the others.

The man Loki had an eating contest with was none other than fire itself. Thjalfe had raced with Utgard-Loki's thoughts, and it was not easy to beat the speed of the racing mind. The horn Thor had drunk from was the sea itself. It was almost a wonder to see how Thor drank so that the sea itself diminished and the ebb and flow came into being. The cat he had lifted was none other than Jörmungandr, and the old foster mother the aging process personified. When he heard this, Thor seized the hammer in anger to crush Utgard-Loki, but both he and his farm had vanished. This story tells how the individual consciousness is helpless against the violent cosmic forces that exist in the collective consciousness.

It is no use applying the laws of individual consciousness to the home field of collective consciousness. Here, one must know and follow the rules of the game or be deceived. In this reality, neither Thor's strength nor Loki's cunning were useful. Here, we find ourselves in a world of primal energies and symbols.

In a way, we can say that Utgard-Loki's halls are the places we visit when we dream. Here, shapes and symbols can change and be exchanged without regard to time and space. Here, the individual consciousness encounters a world of essence, completely different from the usual ordered and structural reality it has around it in the waking state. At the same time, this story tells us about both the tremendous powers we, as individual consciousnesses, have at our disposal and how helpless we are in the face of the tremendous forces in the cosmos. We also learn that Utgard-Loki treats his guests nicely when they are on his turf, even if they are helpless.

The collective psyche is not trying to wipe out the individual consciousness. The final goal of the jötnar is still hidden, and as we shall see, there are many indications that it essentially coincides with the goals of the Æsir. I have previously mentioned the jötnar having a connection with Pluto. They represent the unstoppable movement of matter, which inevitably leads to constant change and which constantly threatens the orderly cosmos. In science, it is called the law of entropy.

The Jötnar, the Renewing Force

In Greek mythology, one side of Pluto—Pluton—was known as the god of wealth. We see how the jötnar also possess great and priceless values. The Æsir collect much of their wealth from the jötnar's treasury and Jötunheimr. The jötnar are the very primal force and the cosmic will from which the Æsir descend and must constantly connect to draw renewed energy. As I said, even Odin, with all his knowledge, cannot stop the world's movement towards Ragnarök. The jötnar, the Pluto forces, can probably allow themselves to be defeated a little here and a little there. But they are an eternal current that can never be stopped.

In the story of Loki and the builder, we learned what the consequences would be if someone managed to protect themselves entirely against this energy. Everything would be locked into lifeless structures that would eventually fall apart. Seen from this angle, it is the lack of change, the exclusion of the Pluto energies—the jötnar—that leads to the only real death. A death that is stuck energy, trapped in motionless and stiffened structures.

There is another story about Utgard-Loki that clarifies the connection with Pluto energy. The story, *Gesta Danorum,* originates from Saxo Grammaticus and begins with a Danish king, Gorm, being saved from a sea famine by praying to Utgard-Loki, a power unknown to him.[21] Afterward, Gorm began to ponder who Utgard-Loki was and sent his best man, Thorkill, to look him up.

Symbolically, the myth tells us that the individual consciousness, represented by Gorm, has been in trouble but saves itself by making contact with the deep layers of the subconscious, represented by Utgard-Loki. Now, the individual consciousness will reestablish contact with the deeper layers of the psyche and direct its searching Jupiter energy—Thorkill—inward to trace this layer of consciousness.

Thorkill equipped a good ship and set off on a longer journey through the interior landscape. He first met two ugly trolls who told him the way to Utgard-Loki. Eventually, they found a cave crawling with worms and lizards. Deep down in the cave, they found Utgard-Loki, half sitting, half lying, and chained to the wall. The stench was almost unbearable.

Here, we see how psychic material has been left in the subconscious and rots. The jötnar, the Pluto energies, have been repressed and controlled and have not been allowed to emerge into the daylight of consciousness. In Norse mythology, Loki was to be chained to a cliff when Ragnarök approached. We see again how our logic and reason bind the primordial forces in the psyche but, at the same time, block their own unfolding—precisely because these primordial forces are bound. The result, as mentioned in the tale, is a terrible stench in the depths of consciousness from all the repressed impulses.

Thorkill broke off a strand of beard from Utgard-Loki's chin, releasing the stored energies. By then, the stench had become so terrible that many of his men dropped dead. On the way out of the cave, they were attacked by flying worms that spewed poison at them. Meeting Pluto's forces is not easy

---

21 J. Orlik and H. Ræder (ed.), *Saxo Grammaticus: Gesta Danorum* (Copenhagen, 1931).

when the jötnar run free nor when they are chained deep below the surface. For those versed in Greek mythology, it can be interesting to make a comparison to *The Odyssey* by Homer.

Not many of the Thorkill's men survived the meeting. Most of the illusions of consciousness and ego, represented by Thorkill's men, die in the meeting with the truth of this stench. But Thorkill, the optimistic Jupiter energy, survived and took the hair back to old King Gorm.

Kings are associated with the center of individual consciousness. In this case, the material that Thorkill brought with him from the subconscious became too much for the king and closed the book of his life. Again, we can see how Pluto's power acts, purifying and transforming. The material brought up from the stinking subconscious causes the old way of experiencing the world to die so that a new king can rise. The reason it stinks so much is that the old king—old consciousness and ego identity—had been in power for far too long.

THOR IN GEIRRÖD'S FARM

There is one more story about Thor that I would like to mention. Once, Loki had changed himself to a bird that teased and mocked a jötunn named Geirröd.[22] But in the end, it went wrong, as it often does for Loki. One of the bird's legs got caught in a net, enabling the jötunn to capture him.

Birds are associated with thought and the Air element. Loki represents the mental processes that are absorbed by the forces of the subconscious and cannot be released. It can be dangerous to play with such violent forces hidden in the psyche. Geirröd starved Loki, in his bird form, to get him to identify himself. This situation occurs when we are no longer able to separate our thoughts from the collective primordial force when we are gripped by anxiety and helplessness. To be

---

22   Anthony Faulkes (ed.) and Snorri Sturluson, *Edda: Skáldskaparmál* (Viking Society For Northern Research, 1998).

set free, Loki must promise that Thor will come to Geirröd's farm without weapons.

In this situation, Thor can't rely on his preferred methods of violence and force to help his fellow god. Here, Thor, with his deep Jupiterian faith, optimism, and ability to find solutions when everything looks bleak, must face the terrifying forces of the subconscious without his usual weapons. It is not about fighting to conquer new land or defeating the jötnar who have entered Asgard. Here, there are parts of the divine individual consciousness that have been captured and held fast in Jötunheimr's dark realm.

We recognize some aspects of this situation from the tale of Thrym. There, too, Thor had to use unorthodox methods to retrieve his beloved hammer. Thor set off for Geirröd's farm to rescue Loki from the clutches of the forces of chaos. On the way, he visited a jötunn woman named Grid. The jötunn woman would eventually become the mother of one of Odin's children, Vidar. He was the one who, at Ragnarök, finally killed the raging wolf Fenrir.

Grid stands for the fertility and peaceful beauty found in the primal force. That it is her and Odin's son who defeats the wolf is no coincidence. Vidar is the son of the faith and cunning of the individual consciousness and the generous fertility of primordial power. This combination proves to be more powerful than the ferocious fury of Fenrir the wolf. Grid lent Thor a strength belt, a pair of iron gloves, and her walking stick. She thought he could use them in the meeting with Geirröd. These are weapons that those who must go out in battle against anxiety and discouragement can use.

Along the way, Thor must cross a violent river. When he was in the middle of the river, it grew and became so foaming and huge that it beat over his shoulders and threatened to topple him down. Then he looked up and spotted one of Geirröd's daughters standing broad-legged across the river and increasing the water masses with a stream of urine. Thor grabbed a large stone, threw it at her, and said, "Power must be voted on at its source."

The rock struck Geirröd's daughter just where she was peeing from, and the river immediately calmed down to a trickle. This flow of urine that threatened to drown Thor is the flood of what is impure, undissolved waste matter in the world and ourselves. We encounter these energies when we move into areas where anxiety and uncertainty prevail. Thor did not let the feeling of standing up to his neck and drowning in waste discourage him. He blocked the polluting current of worry and doubt and thus managed to keep his head above water.

A MISERABLE ACCOMMODATION

The next challenge on this journey of trials came when Thor finally arrived at Geirröd's farm. There, he was first welcomed into the goat house, where there was only one chair. Being received in the house where the goats live represents a low level of respect and self-identity. As he sat down on the chair to rest, it was lifted toward the ceiling. Consciousness is about to become ungrounded. The problems and the low self-esteem feel like the roof coming down on his head, pressing him to the ground.

To avoid being crushed, Thor placed his walking stick against the ceiling beams and pushed away. He refuses to be broken. Then, howling and screaming emerged from beneath the chair. Geirröd's two daughters, Greip and Gjálp, had been sitting there, and now he had broken both of their backs. With the help of his will not to be stopped by adversity and difficulties, Thor had managed to overcome feelings such as hopelessness and discouragement.

Thor's self-respect began to increase, and he was in good spirits when he entered Geirröd's hall. Now, the jötunn challenged him to a test of strength. Geirröd grabbed a red-hot iron bolt with pincers and hurled it at Thor. The iron bolt represents glowing rage and anxiety that had been simmering in the subconscious for a long time. Thor, wearing the iron glove given to him by Grid, caught the iron bolt. Geirröd ran and hid behind a pillar. Thor did not hesitate and hurled the bolt through the pillar, through the jötunn, through the wall, and deep into the earth outside.

This describes the same principle of karma, but it is seen from the opposite angle. When Thor uses his hammer, it always returns. He must face the consequences of his own actions. Here, he used the iron glove to hurl the glowing bolt back at Geirröd. He used the power of strength and desperation of the negative forces in the psyche to dissolve them, and he sent the consequences of Geirröd's actions back to Geirröd.

As Geirröd was pierced by the bolt and had now disappeared, the ordeal was over. The iron bolt that penetrated the earth shows that problems are grounded and buried. Hope and the orderly cosmos have once again triumphed over the fear and dread of being engulfed by chaos and darkness.

HEIMDALL AND SATURN

Heimdall is the guardian of the orderly cosmos. Is there any simpler way to describe Saturn? The Greek Kronos, Saturn's role model, was, in the same way as Heimdall, the guardian of the gods at the celestial axis. Kronos (also spelled *Chronos*) is associated with time, as in the idea that things that follow each other are in chronological order. The universe Heimdall guards is a world within the framework of time and space, a world that is manifested on the physical level.

In astrology, Jupiter and Saturn are often seen as a couple. Where Jupiter stands for opportunities and openings, Saturn stands for trials and duties. By looking at the difference between Thor and Heimdall, we can gain an important new insight into how these energies work in our lives. We have learned that Thor's main occupation is fighting against jötunn. Thor operates as the warrior within our own psyche. He fights against blockages and threatening elements that rise in our consciousness. Thor—Jupiter—is thus concerned with removing what prevents us from going out and conquering the world. He represents energy that helps us see possibilities and overcome resistance within ourselves.

Heimdall, for his part, is concerned with creating order and structure in the outside world. We can say that Thor takes care of the preparatory work and opens the doors, while Heimdall shows us how to learn to master the rooms Thor opens for us. It is important to note that Heimdall is not an unimaginative toiler. We remember that it was Heimdall who, in the story of Thrym, had the idea of how to win back Thor's hammer. It is very often Heimdall who offers good advice when discouragement and hopelessness overwhelm the gods. The power we have conquered through mastering the outer world helps us face adversity within.

As we shall see, Heimdall is strongly linked to people's mastery of physical reality. It is said that Heimdall's strength is increased through the power of the earth. In astrology, this is experienced through the fact that the more we have contact with and master physical reality, the easier access we have to the energy that Saturn represents. Heimdall's home is called *Himinbjörg,* meaning "sky mountain," and from there, he watches over Bifröst, the rainbow bridge between Earth and the realm of the gods.

THE TEACHER

Heimdall sits by his castle and keeps guard of Bifröst and the human world. Similarly, the planet Saturn guards the boundaries of the world limited by matter. Odin or Ouranos has created the world and is bound to it, but on a completely different level than Heimdall. The Bifröst is the bridge that the dead, who were going to Valhalla, rode by. It is the link between earthly and spiritual life. The fact that Heimdall has this place in Norse mythology coincides entirely with the fact that this god psychologically has the same function as Saturn in myths and astrology. The big difference is the positive relationship we have with Saturn in countries far to the North, where we need to plan our lives and have proper houses to live in if we want to survive the cold of winter.

Nothing escapes Heimdall. He sees as clearly at night as he does during the day, needs less sleep than a bird, and can hear the grass growing. In other words, there is no point in cheating or fantasizing when dealing with these energies. You can deceive yourself, but the truth about what and who you really are, what you have done, and where you are in your own development process will inevitably come to light sooner or later.

Heimdall is the strict teacher who reveals how much you really know and can do. Nothing escapes the guardian of the rainbow bridge. Whoever is going to ride over Bifröst must be ready for it. What is manifested in time and space must follow the laws that exist within time and space, the law of karma. One of the reasons for being in the limited physical reality is, as we shall see, precisely to learn how to master these laws in order to thereby develop our individual consciousness and potential. Norse mythology deals with a phase in cosmic development history, which is linked to the development and clarification of the self.

Ragnarök, the end of the world, is, as we shall later explore, not total doom and destruction but a transition. An interesting point is that Loki and Heimdall will kill each other at Ragnarök. The finite thought and the destiny of the manifested world are inextricably linked. It is said that Loki and Heimdall fought each other in the form of seals in the primordial sea at the dawn of time. Thought has always tried to defeat the framework that the created universe builds up around it. But at the same time, the form of consciousness that Loki represents is, by its nature, necessarily limited. Seen from this level of understanding, Loki and Heimdall represent manifestations of energy conditioned by physical reality, limited by time and space.

Neither of the two nor any of their sons and daughters will return to the new world that emerges after Ragnarök. Their energy will be understood in completely different ways when the world is seen from a more universal and mature perspective.

THE WHITE GOD

Throughout Norse mythology, Heimdall is seen as having special significance for humans. He is never perceived as a difficult or unpleasant energy. On the contrary, he helps people develop their abilities. It should not surprise anyone that cultures that emerge in the cold climate zones have a positive relationship with Saturnalian energies. In these areas, we need to develop tools for hunting, fishing, and farming in order to cope with the harsh conditions that nature offers.

Heimdall is also called the "white god" and the "brightly shining one." For me, these names are associated with several things. One interpretation is that he is associated with winter and the white snow and cold that this season represents. Additionally, he corresponds to the calm, quiet, and peace that it brings, the calmness that descends on people when they are safe inside when the cold of winter is outside. Heimdall teaches us to see clearly. Through experience, we learn. By mastering Heimdall's tasks, we gain clairvoyance and thus help sprinkle the created world with light.

In the spring and summer, the Vikings went on raids to the east or west. During the winter, they sat at home and prepared for next year's unfolding. One of the things Heimdall—Saturn—teaches us is to wait, as well as to prepare thoroughly. By gathering energy within ourselves, we can go out and master the world. This inner silence is also reflected through the story of Heimdall's sound, perhaps his hearing, being buried under the World Tree.[23] In winter, the sounds are buried under a white blanket of snow. It also says something about Heimdall's energy being bound by the created world.

The World Tree is a symbol both for humanity (the microcosm) and the manifested universe (the macrocosm). Only when Ragnarök comes and the World Tree falls will Heimdall's hearing be released. Only when the process is complete will the energy that is bound to the physical world be released.

The myth says that just before Ragnarök begins, Heimdall will blow the Gjallarhorn and notify the other gods that the time for the final battle has come. The tunes coming from Gjallarhorn are Heimdall's sound, his hearing set free. Maybe it's a cry of pain from being tied up for so long. Perhaps the sound from Gjallarhorn contains anxiety about what is to come, pain over what has been, and joy at finally being set free.

Loki, who becomes Heimdall's bane in the final battle, has also been chained and is waiting for Ragnarök. They are both associated with human constrictions. Loki represents the desperate suffering and loneliness of thought, while Heimdall

---

23   Arthur Gilchrist Brodeur (trans.) and Snorri Sturluson, "Gylfaginning," *The Prose Edda* (American-Scandanavian Foundation, 1916).

is a symbol of stoic calm. It is Heimdall who takes his lonely fate as the guardian of the gods at the outer limit of the world with composure. And as I have said, both will cease to exist after Ragnarök. The experience of the physical world as a limited space and the lower mind that imagines our soul having the ability to die will cease at Ragnarok. These energies, which in astrology are symbolized by Mercury and Saturn, will act in such a different way after this transformation that they will have almost nothing to do with their old forms.

We will perceive what we call "reality" in a completely different way so that the understanding of these energies becomes something completely new. It will be a gift for the soul to have thought and individual consciousness and to exist in the material world. Presumably, we will become an integral part of a completely new entity than the one we know today.

When we read the myths, we can feel and sense Heimdall's longing for this level of realization. When the time comes, we will have understood more of the purpose of humanity's journey through time and space. But since Heimdall is one of the wisest and most far-sighted of the Æsir, he knows that such freedom cannot be realized until humanity is mature enough to take this great leap in the development of consciousness.

We recognize astrological Saturn's seriousness and its longing to become the master of all so that one can be set free. Patience and self-discipline are necessary for this to become a reality. But let us return to the present world of humanity. A myth called "Rigsthula" addresses Heimdall's kinship with humanity.[24] According to this myth, we are all actually the sons and daughters of Heimdall. We get another clue as to why Heimdall and Loki must disappear from the world of the gods after Ragnarök, which is that they will be fully integrated into the consciousness of humanity at this stage of the evolutionary process.

---

24   Henry Adams Bellows (trans.) and Snorri Sturluson, "Rigsthula," *The Poetic Edda* (American-Scandanavian Foundation, 1923).

Perhaps you are used to thinking of humanity as a product and as an end result, but I urge you to think differently; instead, try and see people as a stage in a process. A cosmic consciousness development process, where what we struggle with at the moment is only one link in a long chain.

HEIMDALL ON A VISIT TO THE HUMAN WORLD

According to "Rigsthula" in *The Poetic Edda,* Heimdall went to visit the world of humanity, and he wandered the Earth. One day, he stepped into a couple's wretched cabin. They are referred to in the story as "great-grandfather" and "great-grandmother." He was offered what little food they had in the dilapidated house, a chunky and sweet soup. Heimdall stayed there for three days and three nights and gave them good advice. Nine months later, she gave birth to a son who was named Thrall (meaning "slave"). He had wrinkled skin and big fingers. Thrall worked and toiled from morning to night, but luckily, a sunburnt woman with mud on her feet and a crooked nose arrived. Her name was Thir (meaning "slave woman"). Thrall and Thir mated, becoming the origin of the race of serfs.

Heimdall made a round trip during his journey through the world of humans. He continued his travels and came to a hall. Another couple were sitting inside. They owned their own house and were clean and well-kept. The couple, referred to as "grandfather" and "grandmother," cooked a delicious calf for the renowned guest, an experience much different from the one he had with the elderly couple before. Heimdall gave them good advice and stayed there for three days and three nights. He settled down between the two of them in the double bed. Nine months after the visit, grandmother gave birth to a well-built child who was given the name Karl (meaning "freeman"). He married and settled with his wife, Snor. Together, they birthed the race of craftspeople and farmers.

It may seem as if Heimdall was in a rush as he continued straight ahead until he came to a large hall. The man in the house took care of his weapons, and the wife was very nicely dressed. They are referred to as "father" and "mother" in this tale. Heimdall also had a lot of good advice to give to this well-groomed couple. True to his habit, he settled down between the married people in the bed. After three days and three nights, he traveled on once more. Nine months later, the mother gave birth to a son who was given the name Jarl (meaning "earl").

Heimdall came by the house of mother and father now and then to take care of Jarl's upbringing and teach him many of his secrets, including runes. As an act of ownership, Heimdall even gave the boy his own name (Rig) at a later time. Jarl married Erna (meaning "the shining one"), and together, they became the origin of a family of chiefs and rulers. The youngest of their sons was named Kon the Young or *Konr ungr* (meaning "the young king"). The very word *king* is probably derived from this tale.

From Vedic mythology, we know about the division of people into castes. Some are born to be enslaved, and others are born to rule. But if we look at this division as part of a process, it says something completely different. In Heimdall's first encounter with physical reality, the human consciousness presented Thrall and Thir. They are dependent on and enslaved by nature. Tools, techniques, industry, and data have not yet been developed. Humanity is dependent on nature's whims and generosity. Consciousness has not been developed to the level where humankind begins to intervene and control its surroundings. But eventually, people begin to master the world around them.

After dependency on the bare essentials granted by nature, we arrive at the next stage of human consciousness. We emphasize that it is a process where Heimdall first visited great-grandmother and great-grandfather, then grandmother and grandfather, and finally, mother and father. We can see this process on two levels: as a common human development and as the process each of us goes through as individuals.

Karl, the son of "grandmother" and "grandfather," is a free man. Humanity has learned to use nature; it is no longer helplessly at the mercy of its surroundings. As free people, we govern ourselves to a large extent but still have limited resources and must strive to keep the goods we have achieved.

Mother and father's son, Jarl, stands for the next step of human consciousness along with the luminous Erna. Heimdall has taught Jarl runes, which has given him an awareness of the world, the power of thought, and the ability to create. In their world, resources are not limited but a source to be drawn from. They have learned to rule over the created reality and are no longer bound by the struggle to survive. Their energy has been through the two previous stages in the process and is thus free to be used for other things. From this starting point, the artist and the mystic begin their journey. It is for those who seek beyond the physical and into the essence of the force.

THE CORONATION OF CONSCIOUSNESS

Kon the Young stands for being king in and over his own consciousness. He has learned runes, can save lives, knows how to blunt the edge of swords, and can calm the sea. It is worth noting that Kon the Young masters many of the same things as Odin-Uranus. At this stage of development, the human consciousness has made contact with its own intuition and spiritual insight. The young man can speak many languages fluently and has great inner calm. He understands the language of nature, dares to compete with Heimdall in runic art, and even beats him.

Human consciousness has now mastered the limited world that Heimdall watches over, which is also the old world of the gods. This awareness opens something completely new and extends far beyond the old. That is why Kon the Young beat Heimdall in the rune contest. The poem says it like this:

> *There he won the right and sovereignty*
> *Over Rig's name and the rune lore.*[25]

---

25   The author's translation of Snorri Sturluson's "Rigsthula," *The Poetic Edda*.

Rig, in this context, is one of Heimdall's names and means "father." That Kon the Young got the right to this name means that the human consciousness had become aware of its origin and creative power. That the consciousness we spring from—our father—is housed in our own psyche. But Kon was still bound to the created world. The poem continues:

> *Through thickets and forests*
> *Let the arrow fly*
> *And the bird fell silent*
> *Then a crow said*
> *Sat on a twig*
> *Why do you silence*
> *Birds Kon-Unge*
> *Rather you should*
> *Spur on the horse*
> *Draw the sword*
> *and beat enemies.*[26]

That Kon the Young caught birds means that instead of listening to intuition, he played with thoughts and didn't listen to the sound from the true messengers. The crow that spoke to him represents intuition and clear thought. Crows were considered to be messengers from the spiritual world, especially from Odin (Uranus). What the crow encouraged Kon the Young to do was to ride into spiritual battle. The purpose was to fill up Odin's feast table in Valhalla with spiritual warriors. They were part of Odin's plan to make the gods as well-equipped as possible for Ragnarök.

In its ultimate consequence, the crow told the kings among men, represented by Kon the Young, that it was time to prepare for the battle of Ragnarök. This is the last great battle where the self will perish in order to emerge as something completely new. Viewed in relation to Saturn's

---

26   The author's translation of Snorri Sturluson's "Rigsthula," *The Poetic Edda.*

mode of operation in the horoscope, we can see how the Saturnian energy constantly seeks to develop us. But it also shows how we tend to get stuck in structures after we have mastered them. If the young man hesitates to listen to the birds, it is neither our integrity nor our wit that does this but our way of using it. We can say that the combination of Heimdall and Loki leads to this. Heimdall gives us tasks to learn, and Loki gives us the necessary tools to learn them, but at the same time, it prevents us from having the necessary inner confidence that makes us dare to let go and move on.

Heimdall is a wise and beautiful god. Images of the planet Saturn have shown us incredible orderly beauty, with bands upon bands of the most beautiful forms of energy orbiting around a fixed center. Seen from this angle, Saturnian energies are not the ones that block our journey through the realm of consciousness, but on the contrary, they are the very tools we need to walk this path.

NJORD AND NEPTUNE

THE GODS OF FERTILITY AND UNCONDITIONAL (AND CONDITIONAL) LOVE

In a time before this time, there was a war between Æsir and Vanir. After long and hard battles, they decided to make peace. As a guarantee for this treaty of peace, they gave each other hostages. The Vanir gave Njord the Rich and his two children, Frey and Freya, as hostages to the Æsir. These were shown honor and dignity and taken into the circle of the Æsir on an equal footing with the other gods.

The Vanir represent a completely different power than the other Norse gods. While the Æsir are linked to the development of consciousness, the Vanir represent the emotional side of existence, and the war between Vanir and Æsir is the conflict between feelings and thoughts in all of us. As I have touched on before, when something happens in the myths, it happens because it must happen. It is a poetic way to describe the laws of the universe as they are rolled out into action. In humanity and the gods' effort to resolve the conflict between mental and emotional impulses, feelings were subsumed into consciousness. The Vanir were hostages of the Æsir. They were held in high esteem but were still in a foreign dimension. We can see how this corresponds to the emotional situation of the vast majority of people who don't live in a natural society.

The war between the Æsir and the Vanir also refers to the transition from societies where the feminine and collective consciousness were dominant to societies where the individual and masculine principles are more strongly emphasized. Before I go on, I will briefly touch on our perception of the planetary energies as they work through the horoscope. We look at and interpret these giant energy centers from our own cultural and personal reality.

We interpret the world through the eye of our ego or self. The process we find described in mythology is very much the story of the self, the development of separate individual consciousness. Seen from this point of view, each planet and god has an energy of certain qualities that we describe as either "good" or "bad." But what we describe in this way is not the essence of planetary energy but our experience and application of it at our current stage of development. That is, for the vast majority of us, as it appears from the small peephole of separate individual consciousness. In reality, the essence of everything just is. It is neither good nor bad; it simply *is* without judgment placed on its value.

Emotions, on the other hand, connect us to others. They exceed the boundaries of the ego but do not necessarily lead us to cross these boundaries. For example, I can feel love for a dog. Emotionally, I am then outside of my limited ego reality, but my consciousness is still connected to the self that feels this love. We see how emotions have a quality that consciousness is unable to grasp as long as it is inside the separate ego. As mentioned before, the Vanir are hostages in an unknown land. They are, in their original nature, connected with collective energies.

Among the Æsir, the Vanir have taken on a different function than they had in their own circle. The myths about Njord's son and daughter, Frey and Freya, probably arose when the peace between the Æsir and the Vanir was created. The pair of them are linked to emotions, attraction, and lust, which are with the individual consciousness. They are linked to Mars and Venus, as these planetarian energies are experienced by the separated individual. They stand for personal love and passion, but there is always a longing for what does not yet exist and is visible in these two gods and planets. It is a longing to be absorbed into a greater unity, to lose oneself in the intoxication of love or victory.

We can say that Freya and Venus carry with them memories of the great collective sea of emotions, which is still Njord's domain. Njord is in a slightly different position. While Frey and Freya are connected to the energies of Mars and Venus, planets which, in ego-oriented astrology, are linked to the individual's emotional needs and will, Njord is the Nordic people's representative for Neptune. He connects us with an energy that remains difficult to understand for the individual consciousness. He was born and raised in another culture and will always be characterized by this. In other words, Njord has immigrated at a mature age, while Frey and Freya have come to the land of the Æsir as relatively nondescript immigrant children.

The Vanir are linked to fertility and human bisexuality. It is said that marriage between brother and sister was a common custom among the Vanir. Symbolically, this means that they guard the secret of humanity's bisexuality. Freya is also the one who teaches other gods and humans about seidr. In seidr, the person doing the magical work must often be able to shift gender and be involved in sexual acts that diverge from the binary gender. This is linked to a point in history when reproduction and sexuality were still a collective matter. The children of a community were not necessarily attributed as belonging to the parents, nor did parents have special rights or ownership over these children. The children came into being through a collective ritual and were part of the tribe.

NJORD AND NERTHUS

Shortly after the birth of Christ, the Roman Tacitus, in his work titled *Germania,* describes how the people of southern Jutland (Denmark) worshiped a goddess they called Nerthus. Linguistically speaking, Nerthus and Njord have exactly the same meaning. This goddess was driven around the country on special occasions designated by the priests. When she came to visit, all weapons were put away, and peace reigned.

After such a journey, the goddess was taken to a lake and washed by slaves, who were then swallowed by the sea. The fact that the sea swallowed the slaves tells us that Neptune's energies are involved in this tale. The individual who has experienced contact with Neptune's energies—the absolute love or total confusion—ceases to exist as a separate individual for some time and is, therefore, "swallowed by the sea."

Leaving aside the symbolic meaning, it seems likely that the process where the drowned slaves washed the goddess gives us an idea about the mercilessness spiritual adoration can have. A clearer demonstration of what spiritual leaders can do in the name of love is hard to find. The sacrifice and surrender that Nerthus or Njord stand for are linked to the inner plane. Carried out as a concrete action in the external world, it has, through the ages, had unappealing results, such as human sacrifice and the like.

It is disputed whether Njord and Nerthus are siblings who were married to each other or whether Njord is a continuation of the Nerthus figure. For me, this is not a significant conflict. Njord and Nerthus represent sides of the Neptune energy that cannot be separated; one always accommodates the other. In the same way, unconditional love accommodates most things.

Njord is a withdrawn god among the Æsir. He is called "Njord the Rich" and intervenes very little in the actions that take place. These forces do not intervene in daily life when looked at from the point of view of the separate individual consciousness. You can still go to Njord and ask for his assistance. He can calm the sea and give you wealth and peace, generally helping you to overcome all physical shortcomings.

The struggle of the Æsir is aimed at conquering the world of the jötnar, toward conquering material reality, mastering the world, and developing human self-consciousness. Together with Odin, the main goal for them is to gain the power of wisdom. Seen in relation to this, Njord's principle of love becomes a peripheral energy. The same then applies to Frey and Freya, even if they are more relevant in this quest than their father. Njord rules over the sea, the cosmic sea. He stands for the infinite wealth found in our inner world of experience.

Understandably, Njord was not the one at the front of the queue to slaughter jötunns. He is also called the head and lord of the sanctuary. It is Njord who rules over the places dedicated to the sacred. Places that symbolically represent the opening to a different reality than the human world. Njord lives in Nóatún, which is by the sea. While Heimdall lives at the border of the ordered cosmos, Njord lives at the edge of the great ocean of love, and whoever sets out there will have to let go of something of their individual existence. This concept was exemplified by the slaves sacrificed to Nerthus.

NJORD'S UNFORTUNATE WEDDING

Njord relates to reality in a way that is not much concerned with doing things or being particularly active; however, in one myth, he does take a leading role.[27] He represents what affects reality through symbolism, drawn into the experience through the choices of others. If you want to understand and connect with this energy positively, you will have to actively seek it out. Unconditional and sacred love is something we can move toward but is not something that can be grasped by our hands or heads. The reality of unconditional love tends to appear as we embrace it.

As mentioned before in a tale with Loki, the Æsir had once taken the life of a jötunn called Tjasse. His daughter, Skadi (meaning "darkness"), demanded a fine, and the Æsir agreed to pay it. We understand that the murder of Tjasse had created an imbalance in the world order. The fact that the Æsir agreed to give Skadi compensation for what they had done can be seen as a necessary action to restore that balance. Her first demand was that the Æsir should make her laugh.

Recounting this tale, Loki completed the task by showing the absurdity of the world and making fun of the male genitalia. Skadi represents the Earth's awakening consciousness, the love that grows out of matter. The fact that her father was killed is a sign that the Earth is beginning to become aware of its own existence. A situation that, in many ways, seems to be the state of things today. In the same way that Skadi demanded atonement for damage inflicted upon her, nature today demands reparation for human destruction.

Her second demand was to have Balder, son of Odin, become her husband. As we shall show later, Balder represents the spiritual center of the individual self. In many ways, his role in Norse mythology can be compared to Christ's role

---

27   Anthony Faulkes (ed.) and Snorri Sturluson, *Edda: Skáldskaparmál* (Viking Society For Northern Research, 1998).

in Christianity. Earth and the physical realm will create a connection with the spiritual man in an unbreakable marriage. The Æsir explained that she could not get Balder to become her husband without further ado; she would have to select her husband from the available gods by looking only at their feet. As it is with humans, it is with gods—free will has to be involved. Humanity must choose spirituality and choose a marriage with the rising consciousness of the Earth.

Skadi agreed to these terms. She knew that Balder was the fairest of all the gods and was sure that all she must do to select him as her husband was to spot the fairest feet. The gods lined up, and she studied their feet closely. In the end, she chose the one with the most beautiful feet. She believed they must belong to Balder since everything was spotless about him. But no, it was Njord who had these beautiful feet. In astrology, Pisces, which is linked to Neptune and Njord's energies, rules the feet. The feet are also the foundation we stand on.

Everything is beautiful on Balder, but selfless love is an even more delightful foundation. Though she was disappointed, the wedding between Skadi and Njord took place anyway—this was the deal, after all, and deals have to be kept. That is one of the unbreakable laws in the mythological universe of the Æsir. We see how the feminine Earth energy that existed in the form of Nerthus returns to Njord in a new form. Just as the individual person goes through a process of development, the planet Earth goes through its process as well; as the individual person seeks balance and wholeness within themself, so does the planet.

The wedding between Skadi and Njord was an attempt to heal the division that had arisen between the love of the material Earth and the love of the spiritual and divine. In themselves, they are two sides of the same coin. But the marriage between Njord and Skadi did not go very well—in fact, they argued vigorously. Njord wanted to live by the sea and Nóatún, while Skadi wanted to live in Jötunheimr among the mountains. Desperate for a resolution, they tried for a compromise of nine nights in Jötunheimr followed by nine nights in Nóatún. When Njord finally returned to Nóatún after his visit to Jötunheimr, he was determined never to return. Listening to wolves' howls instead of swans' songs was completely unbearable. The primal power would be too much for the delicate Njord.

It didn't go any better for Skadi when she tried to live by the sea. She could not sleep because of the seagulls' screams and longed terribly for Jötunheimr. In the end, Skadi went back to Jötunheimr, leaving Njord behind in Nóatún. The division of the inner universal love Njord stands for, and Skadi's material and practical love for plants, animals, and everything that is manifested is still strong in humans. It is difficult to avoid experiencing the conflict between personified love and unconditional universal love.

The very word *individual* contains the word *dual.* Everything on this planet is built up of opposites and dualism. The individual is dependent on such a world, where one is set against the other. If there were no differences, the individual would not be able to separate themself from the whole and thus would have to cease to exist as a separate self.

FREY AND MARS

When we explore the myths of Frey and Freya, we move into the area of individual needs and desires. They represent a development from the old Vanir culture, where marriage between siblings was a divine occurrence. In the realm of the Æsir, Frey and Freya have nothing to do with each other on a sexual level. It is forbidden by law. The feeling of total wholeness that Njord and Nerthus had isn't present in these two. Both Frey and Freya are constantly looking for partners and somewhere to express their fertility. Both are strongly linked to the sexual, which is separated from love.

As the individual takes over as the center of consciousness, this happens out of necessity. Sexuality is no longer something humankind only seeks within the tribe to guarantee the continuation of the community and family. As a new individuality emerges, sexuality is experienced as something that lies outside of the concerns of the tribe and reproduction. This is a tricky stage to be in because both Frey and Freya, being fertility gods, have roles to play in order to make the cattle and crops multiply. At the same time, however, they both have individual purposes and agendas.

As previously mentioned, the laws prohibit Frey and Freya from sleeping with each other. What was once one must become two. The laws that maintain individual consciousness depend on keeping the feminine and masculine sides of humanity separate. In the first instance, this is necessary for the ego, or the consciousness of the self, to continue to develop. Humanity must be visible as a single individual instead of just as a member of the tribe. The word *individual* does not only contain the word *dual* but is also connected with something that is indivisible. In a way, it is a duality that can not be split.

It is an interesting journey. First, the two must be separated only to become united again, this time inside the self. From alchemical literature and modern psychology, we know that the moment the masculine and the feminine polarities in an individual merge is called *hieros gamos*—the sacred inner marriage and a new form of consciousness arises.[28]

FREY AND MASCULINE SEXUALITY

Frey is a manifestation of masculine sexual power. He is often cultivated in the form of a penis with an erection. While the god Tyr represents the power of the will as a warrior god, like the Roman Mars, Frey connects to sexual lust, power, and potential. The horse is Frey's sacred animal, and anyone who has seen a stallion with an erect limb will understand why. There is a story about a woman who worshiped Frey in the form of a horse limb laid on flax and onions. It is in the story of Olav the Saint, who Christianized Norway.[29]

In general, the horse represented power and strength. It was used for plowing and clearing the land. The horse had a totally different place in European life and society before the Industrial Revolution. It is not without reason that people still talk about how much horsepower a car has. Through the use of the power that the horse represented, the individual could increase their family, their livestock, and their own influence. The horse also had another important aspect. It was the vehicle used for transporting the dead across Gjallarbrú (Bifröst), and it was over this bridge that they would permanently cross over to the realm of the dead. Some humans and messengers from the Æsir could also use it to cross from one realm into another. From this context, the horse was a symbol

28   The Editors of Encyclopaedia Britannica. "Hieros gamos." *Encyclopedia Britannica*, 3 Mar. 2016.

29   Anthony Faulkes and Alison Finlay (trans.) and Snorri Sturluson, *Heimskringla* (Viking Society For Northern Research, 2011).

of the power that could dissolve the boundary between this world and the hereafter.

It is the same force that is used when doing tantra yoga. If the individual directs the sexual energy inward and toward a different reality than ejaculation in the physical, then the kundalini energy can be awakened and transport the person concerned into another dimension.

Frey and Freya were both connected to the Nordic diviners and priesthood known as *seidmenn:* those who could do magic. We assume that these seidmenn knew that sexual energy could be used for other things than making children and experiencing corporeal pleasure. No matter what kind of ride it was, Frey was considered to be the best rider. The most famous story about Frey is called "Skirnismol," the Ballad of Skirnir.

SKIRNISMOL

One day, while Odin was away, Frey snuck into Valhalla and sat in Hlidskjalf, Odin's throne.[30] He looked all over the world and caught sight of a beautiful girl who lived in Jötunheimr. Her name was Gerd, the daughter of Gymir. Frey thought the girl was so fair and beautiful that he became unspeakably wild and aroused. It was no easy task to get Gerd and bring her to him. She was well guarded in her father's farm, and if Frey should get what he thirsted for, she had to be willing herself.

As it sometimes happens when in love, Frey sat all day and night, pining and longing for his faraway darling. He was sick with heartache, and eventually, Njord decided that his son's torment could not go on any longer. He sent Frey's servant, Skirnir, to Jötunheimr to persuade Gerd to meet Frey. When Frey placed himself in Odin's seat, sexual desire placed itself at the center of consciousness. This is what happens when men think with their lower heads. But it's not enough to go

---

30 Henry Adams Bellows (trans.) and Snorri Sturluson, "Skirnismol," *The Poetic Edda* (American-Scandanavian Foundation, 1923).

and grab what you want. Tactics are needed. The name *Skirnir* means "the glorious one." As Frey's servant, he must be seen as an extension of Frey's energy.

Skirnir mounted his horse and rode out to find Gerd with an energy that is intrinsically linked to our sexuality. Our will and our sexual drives force us to seek outside of ourselves to satisfy the needs within. Through getting to know and having intimate contact with others, we get to know new emotional sides of ourselves. This sitting and longing for the chosen one is also a learning experience. As previously stated, Frey and Freya are two halves of an emotional whole. Since they are separated from each other, they try to satisfy their longing for wholeness through the outer world. Both Frey and Freya have countless erotic adventures. It is as if they seek and conquer all opposite-sex energy in the world around them in order to become whole.

An interesting point is that Skirnir borrowed Frey's sword on the dangerous journey through Jötunheimr, and Frey never got it back. Therefore, when Ragnarök comes, he will become an easy target for the mighty sons of Muspelheim. There is a clear parallel between Frey losing his sword and Tyr losing his hand when chaining the wolf. The wild and unruly power of violence and sexuality must be tamed in an orderly society. In the same way, it must be tamed in each of us if we want to function in a civilized society. Skirnir represents his master's use of consciousness and energy to achieve his sexual and erotic desires.

Knowing what one is doing and developing empathy and an understanding of how things work for others inhibits the unfolding of raw, instinctive power. This is what Skirnir had to do: he needed to understand Gerd's view of the matter and try to get her to agree. Skirnir rode through the raging fire of desire and finally arrived at Gymir's farm. Initially, things did not go according to Skirnir's wishes. Gerd was not at all interested in giving Frey her love and attention. No matter what goodies Skirnir tempted with, her answer was a firm no.

The untouched instinctive and virginal core of the emotional life is not immediately attracted by the thought of giving up its independence. Here, we see a mirrored echo of the Greek myth of Persephone, the young goddess who refused to give up her virginity until she was kidnapped by Hades. Gerd resided on her father's farm, and Persephone was with her mother, Demeter, in the mortal realm. Both were well-protected and had little interest in giving up their virginity. Unlike Persephone, Gerd is already in the underworld, being part of the primeval forces. In Greek myth, Demeter threatened to destroy the world if she didn't get Persephone back from Hades.

Returning to the poem "Skirnismol," Skirnir turned to his last resort and threatened Gerd with a sad and desolate existence if she did not agree to meet with Frey. Skirnir explained that goat's urine would be her only beverage, and she would abhor food. She would be doomed to sit on a gnarled root of trees in the land of shadows where Hel's realm of hunger and pain would be her neighbor. Such would be her fate if she blocked the forces of life from running through her veins. Furthermore, he said:

> *Trolls will hit you all day*
> *You will hump forward*
> *Stagger without meaning*
> *Stagger without aim*
> *You will own tears for happy laughter*
> *Live with tears and sorrow.*[31]

In the same way, Demeter threatened to leave the world desolate if Persephone weren't allowed to return home from Hades. The feminine energy must allow itself to be fertilized for the cosmic order to be maintained: the innocent and virginal must surrender to the fecundating and changing forces in the world so that everything will not be left barren and desolate.

---

31   The author's translation of Snorri Sturluson's "Skirnismol," *The Poetic Edda.*

The Æsir are as dependent on impregnating the jötunn women as they are on keeping Freya away from their clutches.

At the end of this tale, Gerd gives in to the pressure and promises to meet Frey and treat him to tender embraces in a grove called Barri. Frey became wild and giddy with joy and wanted to set off immediately, but Skirnir said that Gerd would not come to the grove of Barri for another nine nights. Then Frey collapsed and said:

> *Long is one night, longer are two;*
> *How then shall I bear three?*
> *Often to me has a month seemed less*
> *Than now half a night of desire.*[32]

It is not easy to be divinely horny and in love but be required to wait for your chosen one. The urge to fertilize, to spread one's seed, so that new generations can be born is strong. Frey's erect penis is a symbol of the life force itself, the urge to secure the future of life, and thus, a kind of eternal life through the continuation of the family runs through his veins. This sense of kinship was particularly important to the old Norsemen. They knew that future generations would respect and honor their ancestors, just as they themselves respected and honored theirs. It shows how this seemingly primitive need for procreation carries within it the longing for eternal life, the urge for the created to continue to exist.

We understand that the Martian force—Frey's energy—has two directions. One is the desire to fertilize the world; the other is the desire to transcend the divide between physical and spiritual reality. Often, the two are mixed, and it feels like divine meaning when we are aroused. If this energy is directed spiritually, the

---

32   Henry Adams Bellows (trans.) and Snorri Sturluson, "Skirnismol," *The Poetic Edda* (American-Scandanavian Foundation, 1923).

primal power will be reined in, and the primeval force will be used to ride over Gjallarbrú instead of covering the mares.

Frey has means of transport other than horses. He owns a schooner called Skidbladnir. It sails just as well through the air and over land as it does on water. The boat can be folded into a small canvas and put in the pocket. When the primal force is used with awareness, it provides energy to travel through different parts of the subconscious. In general, this energy can be used for almost anything. It is up to the user to decide where the ship will travel. The primal force is something that is there all the time. It does not take up any space and can, therefore, be put in your pocket if necessary.

FREYA AND VENUS

Have you noticed that there are many men and few women in the world of the Æsir? Freya is one of two goddesses who has a prominent place among the gods of Asgard. The women are certainly present among this godly race, but they are mostly anonymous compared to the men. What does this tell us? That Norse mythology is sprung from masculine values? Well, the answer is both yes and no. If we look at the last 5,000 years of our history, it is consistently dominated by masculine deities and masculine ways of unfolding.

Before we become outraged over this imbalance, it may be useful to try to understand why masculine energy has dominated so much of our history. It may seem that the development of consciousness is an ongoing cosmic process and that the entire unfolding of the universe is centered around it. By consciousness, I mean something much more than what we, with our relatively simplistic thoughts, perceive as consciousness. It is about moving toward a total understanding of who we are, why we are here, what the universe is, and why it exists.

I would argue that the history of the last 5,000 years revolves around a special phase in this process. Namely, the development of the individual, self-oriented consciousness. The movement has, therefore, been away from the whole. The individual consciousness has had to separate itself from the whole in order to establish its own foundation. The masculine is, in itself, connected to the individual I experience, while the feminine connects us to the whole.

Masculine dominance has simply been necessary for the process of developing a new consciousness, which today's people are partaking in. The fact that masculine gods have dominated in the last 5,000 years is, therefore, not just the result of malicious oppression. In my opinion, it is a dominance that has been necessary for the crystallization of the individual self. My master's degree in the history of theater from the University of Oslo clearly demonstrates how the theater is developed and functions as a mirror of the development of the human sense of having and using individuality.

Norse mythology's main theme is the development of individual consciousness and the movement toward the next step in the process. We remember that Odin is a god who gives everything to find more wisdom and insight. It may seem as if this phase, where the self has been very separate from the whole, is coming to an end in our times. The weight of many full-grown egos is so great that the Earth seems to kneel under the weight of them all. This is one of the reasons why we must pay more attention to feminine energy and restore contact with the whole. In order to restore the imbalance that the development of individual consciousness has created, it is absolutely necessary to use feminine energy in a new way.

It is not a question of returning to a previous state of paradisiacal innocence. Rather, it is of reaching a new stage in the process where the individual consciousness will have a unique center to operate from without being separated from the greater collective consciousness. With this understanding in mind, we return to Freya and the function of feminine energy in Norse mythology.

In this process, one of the tasks of feminine energy has been—and still is—to keep in touch with the collective and, thus, ensure that the individual consciousness does not go completely off the hinges in the unfolding of personal power and strength. Freya, a hostage from another way of experiencing, did not easily adapt to this system, which was built on the principles of masculine energy. Freya is linked to the same powers as love goddesses like Aphrodite and Venus. She represents the desire and longing that lay in the feminine part of the psyche but which seeks to be satisfied on an equal footing with masculine needs.

Freya is based in Fólkvangr (the people's field). She is connected to the people and the masses; of those who die in battle, half go to Odin, the other half to her. Those who die fighting for love naturally come to Freya. It is the warriors of spirit and power who reside with Odin in Valhalla. Freya is mostly concerned with love and beauty. Rumor has it that she has entertained every male Æsir. Well, it is certainly not unthinkable, based on their history and attributes, that she has bedded her brother as well. It was, after all, an old custom among the Vanir.

We recognize the Venusian in Freya's search for sexual pleasure. Freya loves absolutely everything that is beautiful. Two cats pull her cart. The cat is very often a sacred animal that is associated with feminine power. Perhaps this is where the notion that witches and black cats belong together comes from. This beautiful goddess cries tears of red gold. The astrologer in me is tempted to think of the metal copper, which is Venus's metal.

FREYA'S MAGIC POWER

It was Freya who taught the Æsir how to perform seidr (magic), thought it was Odin who knew runes and sorcery. He could manipulate the world from the outside, while Freya influenced the events with another form of magic. The secret of seidr is to enter into things and become one with trees, plants, and animals. The humans that used seidr utilized their will to give desired forces direction from within. It is the feminine and collective-oriented energy that makes seidr possible because we can become one with what is physically outside of us. By accessing parts of our psyche that are connected to collective energies, we can influence things in the outer world.

The driving force behind seidr is emotion. Odin's driving force is his thoughts. He will arrange things specifically because he thinks it is most sensible or expedient, while Freya uses seidr because she desires something. We sense that the power of Venus energy, our magnetic desire, is at least as strong as Frey's power. Frey goes out and fertilizes the world, while Freya attracts whatever she wants from lovers and beautiful things. She draws it in and allows it to grow within her own field of power, like wheat that is growing in a field of land.

The only ones she can't really get ahold of are Odin and her brother Frey, who are forbidden. Odin represents an energy with which it is difficult for Freya to make full contact. Myth says that she is constantly looking for her husband, Od (Odin, perhaps?), and cries tears of red gold in longing for him. This search for Od is Freya's search for the emotional unity that she lost when she was given to the Æsir and the individual consciousness as a hostage. The lost unity with her masculine half (Frey) represents the loss of the old instinctive experience of the whole. The search for Od is the search for a whole that exists on a different level than the individual. Therefore, Freya does not find her long-awaited Od. Only after Ragnarök will the two be able to come together.

Frey is torn between directing his fertility power toward the spiritual or the physical world, and Freya is also divided in her desire. She longs for Od, but, at the same time, all that is beautiful and lovely that can be found in the manifested world is tempting. Not least of all the lovely male gods who, for a moment, can make you forget your hunger for beauty and wholeness, of which she constantly senses the edge. A beauty she never quite manages to reach. It is not so difficult to understand that Freya cries tears of gold, nor is it that she tries to amuse herself as best as she can with the pleasures that are available.

Freya has many names: *Mardöll*, which means "shining sea," and *Gefn*, "the giving," as she was not miserly or petty with her gifts or herself. She is also called *Syr*, "the sow," the feminine power that gives nourishment and fertility to the world.

There are many myths about how the jötnar tried to get their claws in Freya. What would the world have to offer in terms of pleasures if personal desires were swallowed up by the forces of chaos? If there were nothing left to long for? Freya's energies are absolutely necessary if the individual consciousness is going to find some reason to maintain its existence. It is also necessary for us to move forward. Without the longing for something bigger and more beautiful than what we already have, the world's movement toward the unknown would stop. But this energy is a double-edged sword in the same way that Loki's mental energy is. Freya's energies also entail the risk of us being caught up in the temptations of the outside world.

FREYA'S DESIRE

In this myth, Freya acted upon her deepest desire. It explores the story of how she came into possession of the Brísingamen, which is an incredibly beautiful piece of jewelry.[33] Some say that this item was a dazzling necklace set with brilliant stars or a heavenly diadem. The story begins with Freya spotting four dwarfs forging a golden necklace. She became completely entranced with the piece of jewelry and simply had to have it. Freya offered the dwarfs gold and silver, but they answered that they already had enough of such wealth. The only thing that could persuade them to give away this gem would be for Freya to spend a night in bed with each of them.

The four dwarfs represent forces of abundance and light bound in matter. The jewelry represents the incredible riches and abundance that lie hidden in the depths. To bring out the beauty of matter, she must bind herself to it. Only by loving and giving herself to the dwarfs in flesh and blood can she share in the glory. Only through loving that which is embedded in stone and body can we get access to its riches. The experiences that Freya's senses longed for could only be satisfied through the physical world. The story tells us how the body's perception can open up a higher experience and reality. Our senses are also doorways to the divine. We can see a beautiful sunset or hear a beautiful piece of music and feel connected with the divine.

Freya agreed to the conditions. After four nights of activity, the jewelry was hers. The number four is linked to physical matter. It represents the celestial directions, the elements, and our dimension of reality. The four dwarfs can also be seen as the four bodies that the soul drapes itself in when incarnate on Earth: the energy body, the mental body, the emotional body, and the physical body. When the circle was complete, the prize was hers. Freya was overjoyed; she now owned the most beautiful piece of

---

33   Arthur Gilchrist Brodeur (trans.) and Snorri Sturluson, "Skáldskapar-
      mal," *The Prose Edda* (American-Scandanavian Foundation, 1916).

jewelry that anyone had ever seen, but trouble was approaching. Loki had just received news about what had happened.

The lower part of our mental processes interferes with what it might see as Freya's debauched lifestyle. The trickster can turn everything, even morality, into a tool used for its own means. Loki doesn't seem to have any morality in most of the stories told about him, but we often see him condemn others for their immorality. Something that is far too common among humans today. It shows how the intellect would like to have control over Freya's magnetic energy and powers. In order to achieve this, he must involve his blood brother Odin, who is supposed to have access to the wisdom of right and wrong. Odin is the chief, and as it is among humans, the chief's point of view is most often considered the right one by the rest of the pack. Loki is a true trickster and must manipulate Odin into helping him control Freya and that beautiful, powerful piece of heavenly jewelry.

THE AGONY OF CHOICE

Basically, Freya's love game is open and innocent. She is driven by her longing for the beautiful, and she harms no one. But her actions have tied the soul and the erotic to physical matter, which has consequences. Loki tried to sneak into her bedroom to grab Brísingamen for himself, but it didn't work. She was well protected from his tricks and envy of her lush fertility. However, Loki was very persistent, and after a while, he found a hole in the roof of her home. He turned into a fly and flew into Freya's bed chamber. It was not easy for Freya to keep the troublesome fly—representing thoughts—away. The doubts and thoughts buzzed around and tormented her.

Eventually, she managed to fall asleep anyway, and Loki pried off her jewelry and gave it to Odin as proof that she had been fornicating with the dwarfs and wanted him to punish her. The question Odin must decide is whether it is wrong to enjoy physical intercourse with the forces that are connected with these dwarfs. Is there anything here that can be called immoral and sinful? Of course, Odin had his own agenda. When Freya came to Odin and demanded the jewelry back, he replied that there was only one way she could have Brísingamen again. She must turn two powerful human kings against one another. Both of the kings were required to have twenty minor kings under them, who must all go out and fight each other. Even if they fell, their fate would be that they must immediately get up and return to battle until Ragnarök.

Presumably, this wasn't a punishment but the necessary consequence of Freya getting hold of and carrying Brísingamen. Lust and desire have become linked to physical reality and bound to values and beauty that are impermanent and fleeting. Those who fight to become the owner of this earthly wealth will fight an eternal battle. What they gain will be fleeting and perishable. The battle for goods and gold never ends.

Freya did as Odin said. She gave the mighty kings what they needed to start fighting from her cornucopia of desires. After the battle had begun its eternal dance, Odin kept his end of the deal and returned the beautiful Brísingamen. We must keep in mind that Freya was a hostage to the Æsir. The way we see and experience Freya through Norse mythology is linked to the world of the Æsir and their way of thinking. Since the pleasure principle Freya stands for is linked to the ego's pleasure, it must lead to an eternal dance. On the other hand, it is precisely this reality that is the alchemical cauldron for the development of individual consciousness.

When we change our perspective and understand Freya's beauty and pleasure as a collective phenomenon, the perception of this energy will emerge in a new light. Pleasure will no longer necessarily be linked to impermanence or limitation. Instead, it will be attributed to a state of belonging to beauty itself, not an experience of seeing or contacting it as something outside oneself. Then Freya's jewels, Brísingamen, will have been transformed into a shining star inside the hearts of humanity and the gods alike.

FRIGG AND THE MOON

The goal of the alchemist was eternal life, partly gained by the union (*hieros gamos*) of the masculine and the feminine psyches. From Greek mythology, we have learned that the creation of life on Earth began with a wedding between heaven and earth, Gaia and Ouranos. Life as we know it is born out of the meeting between the masculine sky god and the feminine Earth goddess. In astrology, it is not the Earth but the Moon (the Earth's satellite) that is linked to the motherly part of the feminine element. In Norse mythology, Frigg is the companion of the creator god Odin. She is particularly connected to the Earth and to motherhood, which is one of the Moon's specialties.

On one level, Odin and Frigg are heaven and Earth, spirit and matter uniting. But matter is not just a lifeless lump of earth and stone; matter has its own life, which is awakened to consciousness through the meeting with the sky god. Out of matter grows an emotional consciousness. In many ways, Frigg is a continuation of the cow Audhumla, who was the primordial feminine force. Many myths claim that Frigg's father is named *Fjörgynn,* a masculine variant of a name for the Earth. Frigg has grown out of matter and carries the power of matter within her. The Moon and its phases produce tides and thus increase the forces of growth with the Earth. This is how we can understand that Frigg carries both the powers of the Earth and the Moon within her.

ODIN AND FRIGG MEASURE STRENGTH

A legend tells that there was a king who had two sons, Agnar and Geirröd.[34] Frigg took Agnar under her protection, while Odin wanted to help Geirröd. Frigg and Odin competed over who could best help their preferred son. Kings are a symbol of the individual consciousness that humanity is developing. The king's health was considered to be a mirror of the country's health. The king is the individual, and the people are the collective. The question now is, what do we need most in this process? Frigg's feminine power or Odin's masculine energies? The people or the leader, the king?

---

34   Henry Adams Bellows (trans.) and Snorri Sturluson, "Grimnismol,"
       The Poetic Edda (American-Scandanavian Foundation, 1923).

The story goes that one day, the two brothers sailed together in a boat that was heading for their father's farm because the father was dying. As soon as they reached land, Geirröd jumped ashore, pushed the boat out into the waves, and said to Agnar, "Sail wherever the trolls take you!" Geirröd went up to the farm. His father had died, and he became the new king. Geirröd is Odin's favorite. He represents the masculine and individual side of the self that has ruled the world for the past 5,000 years and probably for most of human history. Time passed while Geirröd ruled the kingdom while Agnar fathered children with a jötunn woman in a cave.

The individual consciousness' contact with the feminine is exiled into the dark caves of the subconscious. The part of our individual self that is connected to the collective lies hidden, far away from the clear light of the Sun.

Geirröd ruled for many years when Frigg finally resorted to a cunning ruse. She told Odin that King Geirröd was so stingy with food that people were starving and tormented under his rule. Odin dressed up and visited Geirröd to see if this was true. In advance, Frigg hurried to send a maid to the king with a message that he should take care of a sorcerer who would be coming to the country to harm him. Geirröd, a man of action, bid his men to seize the disguised Odin and chain him between two red-hot fires to make him tell the truth.

The individual consciousness, symbolized by Geirröd, has long been allowed to run free in people. Frigg's intervention shows that a new step in our development is necessary. The lack of the feminine element that Frigg and Agnar represent has led to a lack of the necessary nourishment for the soul.

Geirröd tormented Odin, his higher consciousness, to bring out the truth. One can easily draw parallels between this action and techniques such as asceticism and self-torture or leaders' lack of trust in other people. Now, it just so happens that Frigg's old favorite, Agnar, had been reborn in Geirröd's son, who was also called Agnar. The young Agnar went to Odin with a filled drinking horn. Odin greeted him, recited a poem of wisdom, and revealed himself for who he was.

We can see this as a process. Geirröd's rule was necessary so that his son, Agnar the Young, could take over the throne. The individual consciousness has now built a foundation that enables the more collectively-oriented consciousness to take over the throne. When Geirröd found out who had actually visited, he got up with haste. He ran off to free Odin, but the sword that he had been holding over his knee fell to the floor with the hilt down. At the same moment, Geirröd stumbled, was pierced by the sword, and died.

What the story tells us is that the individual consciousness goes through a change. The sword is linked to the Air element, logic, and the part of the psyche that is separated from the whole. The moment the separated part of the psyche becomes aware of and contacts Odin, the presence of the sky god, it dies. This renewed contact with a greater awareness leads to the individual—the human being—having a new experience of themself, a change that is reflected in the transition from Geirröd the Old to Agnar the Young as king.

Agnar the Young represents the synthesis of the two brothers. He is Agnar reborn, but he is also Geirröd's son. It's a clever story that mirrors Frigg's cleverness as the young Agnar is also a reunion of Frigg and Odin's powers.

The other myth in which Frigg plays a major role is the myth of Balder's death. This story is also linked to rebirth in the same way as the story of Agnar, Geirröd, and Agnar the Young. The myth of Balder, however, is of completely different proportions. The story of Agnar and Geirröd refers to a continuous process where new aspects of the personality are constantly brought out from the dark caves of the subconscious where they have been hidden. The myth of Balder is associated with a violent leap in development. It is about Ragnarök, the doom and resurrection of the known world.

BALDER AND THE SUN

Balder is the son of Odin and Frigg, born out of the synthesis between cosmic wisdom and the power of unconditional love. Balder is the most beautiful of the Æsir; in Balder, there is nothing ugly, neither inside nor out. We have heard the story about the time Skadi wanted to marry Balder but had to settle for Njord. At that time, Balder was not ready for a reunion with the primal feminine forces that Skadi represents.

Balder is the Sun in the horoscope, the brilliant starlight that points to the center of the individual. In the psyche, the Sun is the central point, keeping the other parts of consciousness in their orbits, in the same way that the Sun is the center of our solar system. The inner reflects the outer. Humanity is a microcosm that reflects the macrocosm, and the Sun is the point around which the other planets circle. As we will see later, Balder must share the role of the planetary system's solar symbol with his blind brother, Hod. From the Earth's perspective, the Sun also has two sides, one that we can see and a "blind" side that faces away from the Earth.

Everything with Balder is beautiful; he is the gloriously enlightened self, the part of us that knows our spiritual ancestry and is in touch with our soul. He represents individual consciousness in full contact with its cosmic belonging. We may wonder if Balder, who is associated with the shining Sun, is portrayed as quite passive. The only myth in which Balder plays the main role revolves around his death.[35]

When we see Balder as an expression of our spiritual center, his reticence becomes more understandable. Balder is in touch with his own destiny and the cosmos. He does not, in the same way as the other gods, intervene in the course of the world. Balder does not give birth to karma but has come into existence in the created world and, as a consequence of this, must die in the created world.

---

35   Henry Adams Bellows (trans.) and Snorri Sturluson, "Baldrs Draumar," *The Poetic Edda* (American-Scandanavian Foundation, 1923).

BALDER'S DREAMS

Odin knows that Balder's death is the beginning of the end or, in other words, the beginning of Ragnarök and the end of the known world. The myth tells that Balder began to have nightmares. Odin sensed that this was a foreshadowing of what would happen and that Ragnarök was on its way. Odin would not accept this. With all his knowledge of the world's laws, he tried to intervene and change these developments. There are many indications that Odin's eternal search for wisdom has precisely been to avoid Ragnarök. Odin called together all the Æsir for a council. How could death and the cessation of their existence—and the world's order—be avoided?

The meeting ended with a plan. Frigg was going to make all living things promise not to harm Balder. Fire, water, stones, earth and trees, iron and diseases, poisons and snakes—everything promised to spare Balder. Frigg put everything in touch with the deep understanding that we are all part of the same whole. The created world can never take away our spiritual self, which Balder represents. She knew the tale of the predictions: after Balder's death, Ragnarök and the end of the world would come.

Now, it just so happened that Frigg thought that a tiny mistletoe that lived at the very edge of the world was too small and insignificant to make such a big promise. When the other Æsir heard that nothing could harm Balder, they were happy. They decided to amuse themselves and set him up in the middle of the court to throw spears and shoot arrows at him. Everything bounced off. Balder was invulnerable, and Ragnarök would never come. The individual consciousness will always keep in touch with its sacred essence—at least, the Æsir now believed so. From the human perspective, this means that one who intrinsically understands that every human individual is an immortal spiritual being, regardless of the trials and tests they are subjected to.

In the same way that humans can doubt this intrinsic understanding, there was a doubter among the Æsir. Loki would not believe in Balder's immortality until all methods of killing him had been tried. Loki disguised himself as an old wife and sought out Frigg. With cunning, cleverness, and sly words, Loki tricked her into talking about the little mistletoe at the edge of the world who was too young to make such a lofty promise.

Loki immediately plucked the mistletoe and carved an arrow from it. An interesting technical detail is that it is practically impossible to make something resembling an arrow out of a mistletoe. It is a crooked, parasitic growth that lives on trees. We remember that Yggdrasil, the created world, was depicted in the form of an ash tree and that humankind was created from trees. The mistletoe symbolizes a parasite that feeds on the created world and on humans. In many ways, Loki and the Mercurial energy itself are linked to such a parasitic function. As long as our reason and consciousness serve our higher self, we grow tall and straight. But the moment our lower consciousness begins to produce ideas of our own greatness and attaches to our lower self, it becomes a parasitic growth on the Tree of Life.

BALDER'S DEATH

Loki took the arrow he had made from the mistletoe and went to Balder's blind brother, Hod, who was standing at the edge of the ring. Loki started to chatter with Hod and asked him why he didn't partake in the fun but just loitered in the background. Hod mumbled that Loki didn't need to tease him like that. Everyone knows he's blind and couldn't possibly hit Balder with anything.

"Don't you have bigger problems than that?" asked Loki in his most flattering voice. "We'll arrange that I shall aim if you agree to hold the bow and arrow." As it is said, so it is done.

Hod held the bow and drew the arrow back. Loki aimed. The arrow flew from the string and penetrated Balder's heart. The glorious god sank down to the ground and died. This is a demonstration that Loki alone—pure logic—cannot take the life of Balder by himself. Only by allying himself with Hod, the blind part of the self, was he able to kill Balder. In other words, Loki—representing our negative and tricky thoughts—is able to cut the contact between our individual self and our soul essence. Loki can perhaps be called the "primal atheist," the part of us that doubts everything, including our spiritual origins. Thus, this part of us perceives that the only meaning of life is the one found during the course of a short and limited existence.

This myth is about what happens when contact with our spiritual self is severed. The combination of the lower mind and the blind self has killed the intuitive knowledge of our existence in a spiritual universe. Now, there would be great sorrow among the Æsir. Consciousness is thrown into desperation and the experience of meaninglessness. The created world seems to be an absurd place. What is the point of a glimpse of light in a void of nothingness when the eternal spiritual dimension of the self has been killed? The state of mind after Balder's death is familiar to many in the Western world; the experience of an absurd and meaningless cosmos is depressing and morally degrading.

THE PILGRIMAGE

Filled with sorrow and anxiety, the gods met once more for counsel. They literally set heaven and Earth into motion and tried everything possible to get Balder back. As a start, they sent Hermod, their messenger, to Hel, who rules the underworld where Balder now resided. Hermod pled and investigated whether she could in any way be persuaded to allow Balder to return home to Asgard.

On his ride to Hel, Hermod was exposed to an abundance of dangers and trials. This is the seeker's journey, the path of the pilgrim and the artist. Defying dangers in the inner and outer worlds in the search for something lost deep within ourselves, which we have not yet been able to put into words. It is the longing to get ahold of our own inner essence and discover immortality. When Hermod appeared, Hel was already moved to tears by Balder's beauty. She told Hermod that if everything alive cried for Balder, then he would be allowed to return to the realm of the gods. In the myths, things happen out of necessity. Only a moment of total surrender to our innermost essence makes it possible for the Balderian dimension of consciousness to resume its rightful place in our psyche. It can be compared to our thoughts being full of doubt and preventing us from having total trust in our eternal essence. On one level, the story of Balder's death can be compared to the expulsion of Paradise. It also has clear parallels to the story of Christ, who was killed so that a new world and a new humanity could arise.

Alas, time is set to change, and Balder's death has had irreversible consequences. Odin had fathered a son with the giantess Rind, who killed Hod the day after his birth. This symbolizes that something new was born in human consciousness at the same moment that Hod and Loki killed Balder. Vali, as the avenger is called, represents the longing to restore contact with the spiritual self. He was driven by despair at having lost touch with the pure and perfect dimension of existence (Balder) and rage against the parts of the psyche that had caused Balder's death.

When Vali killed Hod, it was the first time that one of the Æsir willingly took the life of another. The psyche and the ordered world come into conflict with themselves as soon as the spiritual principle in existence is no longer present. The blind Hod, who represents ignorance and innocence, was gone. He allowed himself to be lured by Loki and needed to share his brother Balder's existence in Hel's halls. When what is hidden disappears, the one unable to see it also disappears. There is nothing left to be blind to.

FRIGG'S QUEST

After hearing Hermod's message, Frigg immediately went out into the world. She contacted everything in the world, both biologically alive and inert matter. As the representation of motherly love, she tried to get back what she cherished most in the world. She stands for a deeper principle behind the Moon's astrological significance. In Frigg, we see the longing to regain the innocence and purity that we all once had, what we were before we lost our freedom to Paradise. Here, it was Loki who played the part of the serpent. Frigg tried to find a hidden entrance to that which was gone and lost.

In the Moon, or the collective part of us, lies the yearning to reconnect with the radiant and true individual divine energy that manifests through the Sun. In this tale, it is represented by Frigg's longing to get her son Balder back. The longing of the Moon and the Sun for each other is not directed toward something outside of oneself but toward becoming whole again, much like the individual's longing to return to the security and unity experienced in the womb.

As Frigg stepped into the world, all living things cried when they heard her story of Balder's death. Even the stones and sticks were moved by her grief. Frigg's wanderings are symbolic of the fact that the psyche is now occupied with a deep longing to regain the spiritual center that it lost at Balder's death. All that existed in the world wept because of this longing—almost all. Toward the end of her journey, Frigg came to an old wife, who was none other than Loki in disguise. The wife called herself Thökk, and when Frigg told the story of Balder's death and asked the old woman to cry, she replied: "Thökk cries dry tears."

Loki didn't reject crying because of heartlessness, however. Loki, who represents thought, cannot cry. Firstly, it was he who had caused Balder's death. Secondly, pure mental thought is not linked directly to emotions, which is a prerequisite for tears. Loki represents a part of our consciousness that is not touched by a longing for the sacred. It is the same mental part of us that would rather be right than be well. Loki is as little able to cry as a computer can cry if the user is at home and sick.

Ragnarök is Around the Corner

Frigg left the old wife with unfinished business. Balder remained in the realm of the dead, and Ragnarök was fast approaching. Now came the icy *Fimbulvetr*, the harsh winter that preceded the end of the world. It consisted of three long winters, so hard and so cold that there was no summer in between for respite. Everything froze on Earth—and so hardens the emotional life. The absence of Balder caused hearts to become hard and cold as ice. Balder's heat, which should have melted the endless frost, was bound to the underworld. Humanity no longer saw itself as part of a whole, but rather, each human fought for themselves and their own—a sure path to Ragnarök.

Without the pure energy that Balder represented, the ego went off the hinges. Self-absorption and lack of contact with the whole prevailed. Humanity was no longer aware that the individual self is part of a process and exists for a greater whole, not just to satisfy the needs of the individual. The Solar energy was, in truth, trapped and swallowed up by the lust and blindness of the dark underworld. The consequences of this are described in the great poem or tale of "Völuspá" (the prophecy of the Völva).

> *Brother shall give to brother*
> *Deadly wounds in the fight*
> *Cousins will tear asunder ties of blood*
> *It's hard in the world of men*
> *Whores will reign there*
> *Ax time, sword time,*
> *Shield is shattered*

Wind time, wolf time
Before the world ends
No one spares
Someone else's life.[36]

The Æsir tried to find a way out of their predicament and held a feast to remember Balder. They were very satisfied with the fine service in the halls and graciously praised the servants who provided it, Fimafeng and Eldir. Loki couldn't bear to listen to all of the flattery and took Fimafeng's life in order to stop it. It may seem that Fimafeng is associated with vanity and self-righteousness. In response, the gods simply chased Loki away and went on with their drinking. But after a while, Loki returned to the guild and began to hurl accusations at everyone present.

The mental energy Loki presented is also the energy we use for self-criticism and objective thinking. Loki is the one who can step out of the context of things and lose contact with the whole; therefore, it is Loki who looks at it all from an outside perspective. He can see what kind of faults these gods and goddesses really have.

The gods mourn Balder's death and try to find a way to avoid Ragnarök and the end of their time. But it seems like they themselves have their skeletons in the closet and are, therefore, jointly responsible for the misfortune that has befallen them. The world order Balder was linked to—and which the Æsir represent—was the basis on which the cosmic laws were maintained. Loki's accusations against the other gods are quite strong and indicate that things have been out of balance for quite some time.

---

36 The author's translation of Snorri Sturluson's "Völuspá" from *The Poetic Edda.*

Loki criticizes Odin for having broken his promises from the dawn of time, for having distributed victory and defeat among humans unfairly, and for having behaved like a wretched witch. In turn, all the Æsir try to defend themselves or calm down Loki. But each and every one of them has to listen to Loki's depiction of the ugly truth about their bad sides.

He knows it all and brings up their infidelity, lies, cowardice, wrongdoings, and stupidity. Not one of them is spotless. Everything that has been hidden since the dawn of time is spilling out. With plenty of free time to observe their actions, Loki pokes holes in the gods' self-satisfied images of themselves.

All was far from good in the world, and Ragnarök's arrival is becoming more and more apparent, even acceptable and necessary. The old world had so many errors and shortcomings that it might as well just disappear. The gods had now reached a new stage in their quest to recover what had been lost: the stage of self-examination.

We must see our mistakes and weaknesses if we are to reach a new level of consciousness in much the same way that the gods have to face themselves. They must either change voluntarily or through a Ragnarök of one kind or another. Loki—thought—holds up a mirror to all of the gods so they can choose to become aware of their own faults and weaknesses. The bitterness that lay as an undercurrent in all of Loki's words came from the fact that he did not at all believe that Balder could come back whole or that a new and better world could arise. In any case, the consciousness that Loki represented was bound to perish in Ragnarök. In Loki, we can recognize our own tendency—humanity's tendency—toward self-destructiveness.

Loki was allowed to go on for quite a while, but eventually, his mocking words were too much for the Æsir, and Thor chased him away. It was only Thor, who represents hope and an unfailing belief that anything is possible, who had the power to remove Loki.

LOKI'S PUNISHMENT

The Æsir were eager to take revenge for these insults, and Loki took the form of a salmon and hid in a waterfall to avoid their wrath. After some searching, the Æsir found the waterfall and spotted the salmon. They tried to catch him, but Loki, in his fish skin, was as slippery as an eel. Stopping the flow of negative and self-critical thoughts is not easy, something that everyone who has tried meditation is aware of. Capturing Loki represents this phase in the quest to regain our spiritual essence and to free ourselves from negative mental programs.

Loki, the Mercurian energy, must be controlled so that the psyche can open to the whole. Since Loki would not—and could not—cry for Balder, it became necessary to try other methods to retrieve Balder and for cosmic order to be restored. The Æsir decided to knit a yarn net, as catching Loki required planning and preparation. After much struggle, they finally caught Loki trying to jump over the net. The yarn thus becomes a tool created through purposeful, meditative, and focused work. It forces the Mercury energy up from the emotions it is possessed by so that consciousness can grasp it and keep track of it.

Now came a new problem. The Æsir were filled with powerful emotions, such as hate and lust for revenge, which are not conducive to inner peace or the advancement to a new level of consciousness. Likewise, to hate your own negative thoughts won't do you any good. In their anger, the Æsir bound Loki to a cliff and placed a venomous viper above him. These acts represent the psyche's attempt to rein in the lower consciousness.

Loki's wife, Sigyn, held a dish under the serpent's mouth so that the venom from its fangs wouldn't fall on Loki, but every now and then, the dish occasionally overflowed with fluid, and as she moved to empty the dish, a drop of venom landed on his face. Loki howled and twisted, a ruckus that caused the whole Earth to tremble. Legend has it that this is what created earthquakes.

The mind tries to gain full control over its unruly thoughts, but they twist and turn. A part of us is so connected to this part of our consciousness that we fear the loss of it in the same way that we fear death when our old consciousness is threatened with extinction. We must remember that for Loki, all contact with the whole has been broken. He only had his own existence to live for, and when it was threatened with annihilation, Loki felt as though he would disappear forever.

In this, Loki connects us to our own fear of death and the fear that we exist only as matter in the physical realm. These fears inevitably only lead to suffering, illustrated by the drops of venom from the snake. Loki is unusual, as he is a god who does not believe in the gods. Loki's captivity represents a very distressing stage in the experience of reality where we feel helplessly bound to a foreign and meaningless world, one which must inevitably disappear so that nothing remains.

RAGNARÖK

Now, the world moves fast toward the end—toward Ragnarök. All the world's creatures are set in motion for a great plain called Vigrid. The sons of Surt come from Muspelheim, the world of fire, and the primeval force started to move. The wolf tears its reins. The great worm heaves itself onto the land. Loki's chains become torn asunder. Heimdall warns about the upcoming battle by blowing the Gjallarhorn. Yggdrasil, the World Tree, trembles at its roots, and chaos is unleashed.

The Æsir and all the warriors that Odin had gathered in Valhalla arrived at the fighting ground, ready for battle. Numerous legions sailed from the land of the dead. Many came on the ship Naglfar, which was built from the nails of the dead. Nails, in this context, are associated with claws and greed, a ship built by human avarice. The fierce battle began. Ragnarök was a total mobilization of all energy in the psyche and mind. This was the moment of transition, where the old consciousness disappeared, and a new one was born. Loki's insults, Balder's death, and Heimdall's ride all led up to this inevitable moment, where total consciousness came to the surface.

The wolf Fenrir devours Odin; the pent-up rage eats away at our ability to act on the basis of wisdom and insight. Odin's son

Vidar takes revenge and tears apart the jaws of the wolf with his giant shoe; the strength we have built up through daily and humble work has given us stability that cannot be swallowed up by the wolf's fierce fury. Vidar's shoes are made from the remains that have been collected from everyone who has made shoes and other leather items throughout the ages. Where Odin, with all his wisdom, has to give up, the silent Vidar holds his ground with something as innocuous as his shoe.

Frey went to battle against Surt, the very primordial force from which he had derived his power. Frey had given his sword to Hermod and used his powers to fertilize the earth. Being bound to the created world in this way has weakened him, and alas, Frey falls to the sword of Surt. Heimdall, the guardian of the orderly cosmos, and Loki, who fought each other as seals at the dawn of time, now kill each other. After fierce battles, Thor finally kills Jörmungandr, whom he had fought with throughout many myths. During the fight, the worm spews so much pus and bile at Thor that he falls dead after taking nine steps away from his slain enemy.

Jörmungandr, the Midgard worm, also symbolizes all our unused or unprocessed emotions.

The number nine appears in much of Norse mythology. My interpretation of the number nine, in the context of these myths, is that it always stands for something that leads up to consummation. The number ten represents the result of the first nine steps and, thus, a new beginning. Zero and one are put together again in a new way. We can almost say that the number ten represents a new world order based on the remnants of the old one. When Thor was killed, there was no hope of preserving the old-world order. Now, acid fire is hurled across the Earth by Surt, and the Earth sinks into a sea of flames.

> *The sun darkens*
> *The earth sinks into the sea*
> *In the sky fades*
> *Bright stars*
> *The smoke rolls out*
> *From huge fires*
> *Highly the flames plays*
> *Against heaven itself.*[37]

Then the strange, not to say wonderful, happens. At the same moment that the old world falls, a new one rises.

> *See her coming up the second time*
> *Land from the sea*
> *Eternally dressed in green*
> *Waterfalls fall*
> *Eagle flies over*
> *The one on the mountain*
> *Is fishing*

---

37 The author's translation of Snorri Sturluson's "Völuspá" from *The Poetic Edda*.

Unsown fields will grow
Evil disappear
Balder will be there
Hod and Balder then lives
On Odins battlefield
The sanctuary of the gods:
Do you know enough or what?[38]

Earth gives birth to a daughter as beautiful as herself. This new Earth represents a newly created form of consciousness. Balder and Hod return from Helheim, and contact with the sacred whole has been restored. Hod's blind naivety and trust are united with Balder's luminous figure. The battlefield they inhabit represents consciousness, the field where all the wars had really been fought. This place is the sanctuary of the gods. There, in the grass, they find the lost golden playing pieces from the dawn of time. Once more, the pieces are set up, and the new game begins.

This journey through the darkness of war, conflict, and separation from the sacred essence has ended. Consciousness now sees its own existence and the cosmic process from a completely different perspective. The ego—the individual— no longer experiences itself as a separate and mortal self, which can be obliterated. Instead, it experiences itself as consciousness in eternal movement and change. Time and again, we see Norse mythology as a metaphor for the rise and fall of individual consciousness.

The individual consciousness is developed as a point that can observe the whole. This is how the divine can see and understand itself. Odin has completed his quest for wisdom. Ragnarök is the end of this painful process, which consists of the distillation and development of the individual self. After

---

38   The author's translation of Snorri Sturluson's "Völuspá" from *The Poetic Edda.*

Ragnarök, the individual consciousness will, as mentioned, restore its contact with the whole, a contact that is difficult to lose again. As the seeress in "Völuspá" says at last:

She sees the shining hall
It stands in the sun
With a roof of gold
At Gimle
Lineages without deceit will live
And eternally possess happiness.[39]

---

39 The author's translation of Snorri Sturluson's "Völuspá" from *The Poetic Edda*.

APPENDIX

Gods in Norse mythology in relation to their Greek or Roman counterparts and the planets.

BALDER
Greek: Apollon
Roman: Apollo
Planetary: The Sun

FRIGG
Greek: Hera
Roman: Juno
Planetary: The Moon

LOKI
Greek: Hermes
Roman/Planet: Mercury

FREYA
Greek: Aphrodite
Roman/Planet: Venus

TYR/FREY
Greek: Ares
Roman/Planet: Mars

THOR
Greek: Zeus
Roman/Planet: Jupiter

HEIMDALL
Greek: Kronos
Roman/Planet: Saturn

ODIN
Roman: Caelus
Greek/Planet: Uranus

NJORD
Greek: Poseidon
Roman/Planet: Neptune

HEL AND THE JÖTNAR
Greek: Hades
Roman/Planet: Pluto

BIBLIOGRAPHY

Bæksted, Anders. *Guder og helte i Norden.* Politiken, 1972.

Bellows, Henry Adams (trans.) and Snorri Sturluson. *The Poetic Edda.* American-Scandanavian Foundation, 1923.

Britannica, The Editors of Encyclopaedia. "Astrology Summary." *Encyclopedia Britannica,* 24 Jul. 2021, www. britannica.com/summary/astrology. Accessed 5 Jan. 2024.

———. "Hieros gamos." *Encyclopedia Britannica,* 3 Mar. 2016, www.britannica.com/topic/hieros-gamos. Accessed 7 Feb. 2024.

Brodeur, Arthur Gilchrist (trans.) and Snorri Sturluson. *The Prose Edda.* American-Scandanavian Foundation, 1916.

Doniger, Wendy. "Kali." *Encyclopedia Britannica,* 13 Dec. 2023, www.britannica.com/topic/Kali. Accessed 5 Jan. 2024.

Faulkes, Anthony and Alison Finlay (trans.) and Snorri Sturlason. *Heimskringla.* Viking Society For Northern Research, 2011.

Faulkes, Anthony (ed.) and Snorri Sturluson. *Edda: Skáldskaparmál.* Viking Society For Northern Research, 1998.

Hollander, Lee M. (trans.) and Snorri Sturluson. *The Poetic Edda.* University of Texas Press, 1928.

Holm Olsen, Ludvig (trans.) and Snorri Sturluson. *Edda— Poems.* Further translated to English by Per Henrik Gullfoss, Cappelen Publishing House, 1975.

Lindholm, Dan. *Innsyn i nordiske gudesagn (Access to the Nordic God Legends).* Dreyer, 1987.

Orlik, J. and H. Ræder (ed.). *Saxo Grammaticus: Gesta Danorum.* Copenhagen, 1931.

Rudhyar, Dane. *The Astrology of Transformation.* Theosophical Publishing House, 1980.

Steiner, Rudolf. *Anthroposophical Leading Thoughts.* Rudolf Steiner Press, 1973.

INDEX

A

Agnar, 98–100

Air, 9, 11, 13–14, 18, 27, 31, 36, 43, 52, 56, 88, 100

ancestors, 1, 87

ancestry, 101

Angrboda, 31

Aphrodite, 91

Asgard, 9, 15, 21, 28, 46, 57, 89, 105

ash, 4, 15–16, 104

Astrology, 2–4, 9, 23, 40, 61, 63, 66, 75, 79, 97

Audhumla, 6–7, 97

Aurgjelme, 6

B

Balder, 78–79, 100–111, 113, 116

Baugi, 18–19

Bifröst, 63, 83

Borr, 6

Brísingamen, 94–96

Brokkr, 28

Brother, 6, 13–14, 17–18, 23, 26, 75, 92, 95, 99–101, 104, 106, 108

Búri, 6

C

cat, 35, 52–53, 92

cattle, 81

cave, 55, 99–100

chaos, 7, 13–15, 24, 27, 29–30, 41–42, 45–47, 50, 52, 57, 59, 93, 113

child, 5–7, 23, 31–32, 46, 57, 67, 73, 75–76, 84, 99

Christ, 76, 78, 106

Christian, Christianity, 1, 3, 38, 79

Consciousness, 3–4, 6–7, 9–12, 14, 16, 18–21, 23, 25–33, 35–37, 43, 45–50, 52–58, 61, 64, 66–71, 73–75, 77–79, 81–85, 89–91, 93, 96–106, 108, 110–113, 116–117

cosmic, 3–6, 10, 13–14, 23, 26, 28, 37, 39, 42, 53–54, 64, 67, 77, 86, 89, 101–102, 109, 111, 116

cosmos, 5–6, 11–13, 15, 36, 42, 45–46, 52, 54, 59, 61, 77, 102, 105, 114

cow, 6, 97

creatures, 14, 31, 113

crow, 70

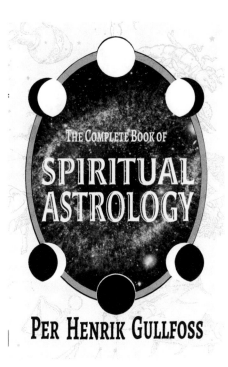

THE COMPLETE BOOK OF

SPIRITUAL ASTROLOGY

PER HENRIK GULLFOSS

The Complete Book of
Spiritual Astrology

Per Henrik Gullfoss

Whether you're new to astrology or a long-time practitioner, this engaging book gives you practical ways to achieve harmony and unity among the body, mind, and soul. Learn how your astrological horoscope is a map that reveals your inner drives, your strengths, and how best to navigate challenges that you may face in your daily life. Set out on your earthly journey towards enlightenment with the sacred wisdom of the stars as your guide.

YOUR STAR SIGN

Per Henrik Gullfoss

Your Star Sign is the second book by Per Henrik Gullfoss, one of Norway's most well-known and respected astrologers. In this book, Gullfoss dives deep into each of the signs of the zodiac, providing a thorough assessment of the signs and how the traits of each can be found to manifest within the individual. Thoroughly researched, beautifully written, and intimate enough to feel as if Per is talking directly to you, *Your Star Sign* is a welcome addition to the Crossed Crow portfolio of books.